Long Time Since Yesterday

A Drama in Two Acts

by P.J. Gibson

A Samuel French Acting Edition

FOUNDED 1830

New York Hollywood London Toronto

SAMUELFRENCH.COM

Copyright © 1984, 1986 by P.J Gibson

ALL RIGHTS RESERVED

CAUTION: Professionals and amateurs are hereby warned that *LONG TIME SINCE YESTERDAY* is subject to a Licensing Fee. It is fully protected under the copyright laws of the United States of America, the British Commonwealth, including Canada, and all other countries of the Copyright Union. All rights, including professional, amateur, motion picture, recitation, lecturing, public reading, radio broadcasting, television and the rights of translation into foreign languages are strictly reserved. In its present form the play is dedicated to the reading public only.

The amateur live stage performance rights to *LONG TIME SINCE YESERDAY* are controlled exclusively by Samuel French, Inc., and licensing arrangements and performance licenses must be secured well in advance of presentation. PLEASE NOTE that amateur Licensing Fees are set upon application in accordance with your producing circumstances. When applying for a licensing quotation and a performance license please give us the number of performances intended, dates of production, your seating capacity and admission fee. Licensing Fees are payable one week before the opening performance of the play to Samuel French, Inc., at 45 W. 25th Street, New York, NY 10010.

Licensing Fee of the required amount must be paid whether the play is presented for charity or gain and whether or not admission is charged.

Stock licensing fees quoted upon application to Samuel French, Inc.

For all other rights than those stipulated above, apply to: Samuel French, Inc.

Particular emphasis is laid on the question of amateur or professional readings, permission and terms for which must be secured in writing from Samuel French, Inc.

Copying from this book in whole or in part is strictly forbidden by law, and the right of performance is not transferable.

Whenever the play is produced the following notice must appear on all programs, printing and advertising for the play: "Produced by special arrangement with Samuel French, Inc."

Due authorship credit must be given on all programs, printing and advertising for the play.

No one shall commit or authorize any act or omission by which the copyright of, or the right to copyright, this play may be impaired.

No one shall make any changes in this play for the purpose of production.

Publication of this play does not imply availability for performance. Both amateurs and professionals considering a production are strongly advised in their own interests to apply to Samuel French, Inc., for written permission before starting rehearsals, advertising, or booking a theatre.

No part of this book may be reproduced, stored in a retrieval system, or transmitted in any form, by any means, now known or yet to be invented, including mechanical, electronic, photocopying, recording, videotaping, or otherwise, without the prior written permission of the publisher.

ISBN 978-0-573-63026-2   Printed in U.S.A.   #14646

Dedicated to the memory of my mother,
Lillian Elizabeth Gibson,
as well as
Derrick Richardson, Jackie Turner, Roddy Gibson,
Ted Pontiflet, Mr. and Mrs. Jackson, Mrs. Minschwaner,
Loretta Devine, Bette Howard, J.L. Grant and Roberta Flack.

Henry Street Settlement's
NEW FEDERAL THEATRE
Woodie King, Jr., Producer

Presents

LONG TIME SINCE YESTERDAY

by
P.J. GIBSON

Set Design by	*Costume Design by*
Charles Henry McClennahan	**Judy Dearing**
Light Design by	*Sound Design by*
William H. Grant III	**Bernard Hall**

Stage Manager
Reginald Arthur

Staged & Directed by
Bette Howard

Premiere October 10, 1985

FOR HENRY STREET SETTLEMENT

Executive Director	*Director, Arts for Living Center*
Daniel Kronenfeid	**Barbara Tate**

This production is made possible with public funds from New York State Council on the Arts, National Endowment for the Arts, New York City Department of Cultural Affairs, the Shubert Foundation and private donations.

CHARACTERS
(In Order of Speaking)

YOUNG LAVEER SWAN............ Sabrina DePina

YOUNG JANEEN EARL .... Ayana Phillips

LAVEER SWAN .... Starletta DuPois

BABBS WILKERSON .... Petronia Paley

ALISA MYERS-REYNOLDS.... Thelma Louise Carter

THELMA CARLSON................. .... Emily Yancy

PANZI LEW McVAIN .... Denise Nicholas

JANEEN EARL-TAYLOR .... Loretta Devine

TIME

LATE SUMMER, THE PRESENT

PLACE

EWING TOWNSHIP, NEW JERSEY

CHARACTERS

YOUNG JANEEN EARL ... A cute eleven year old. A follower. Weak in fortitude.

YOUNG LAVEER SWAN... A cute eleven year old. A maker of dreams come true. Full of fortitude.

ALISA MYERS-REYNOLDS ... Woman of thirty-nine. married. Director of a pre-school program.

PANZI LEW McVAIN ... Woman of thirty-eight. Single. Physical therapist.

THELMA CARLSON.... Woman of thirty-nine. Single. Medical doctor.

BABBS WILKERSON .... Woman of thirty-seven. Divorced. Anchor news person.

LAVEER SWAN .... Woman of thirty-eight. Single. Professional artist/ painter.

JANEEN EARL-TAYLOR. . . Deceased woman of thirty-eight. Married.

LONG TIME SINCE YESTERDAY

ACT I
Scene I

In darkness, the sound of the young JANEEN and LAVEER can be heard singing a child's song.

JANEEN and LAVEER. *(Voice over. Singing.)*
THREE, SIX, NINE. THE GOOSE DRANK WINE. THE MONKEY SPIT TOBACCO ON THE STREET CAR LINE. THE LINE BROKE. THE MONKEY GOT CHOKED AND THEY ALL WENT TO HEAVEN IN A LITTLE ROW BOAT. QUACK. QUACK....... QUACK. QUACK...... QUACK. QUACK...... QUACK.
(JANEEN, singularly continues to sing the "Quack. Quack." portion of the song.)

(The lights rise on JANEEN and LAVEER.)

LAVEER. Wait a minute. Wait a minute. I got a better one.
JANEEN. What? *(LAVEER places her leg up on the porch step. JANEEN sits on the step and watches.)*
LAVEER. *(singing)*
PUT YOUR FOOT ON THE ROCK. SWOOOOO AH. SWOOOOO AH.....

(She does pelvic gyrations on the "Swooooo Ah" section.)
AND LET THE BOYS FILL YOUR.....
(She takes a beat of silence to imply the unspoken word.)
SWOOOOO AH. SWOOOOO AH. DON'T BE AFRAID.
SWOOOOO AH. SWOOOOO AH. 'CAUSE YOUR
MOMMA DID THE SAME."

JANEEN. Oooooo. Where'd you learn that?

LAVEER. *(Proud. She sits beside JANEEN on the step.)* From some girls. Oh, got another one.

JANEEN. What?

LAVEER. *(Singing. Complete with all gyrations.)*
I WANT A PICKLE WITH A BONE IN IT. UNGH. UNGH.....
(Emphasis and gyrations on the "Ungh. Ungh" section.)

JANEEN. Oooooo Laveer.....

LAVEER. What?

JANEEN. That's nasty.

LAVEER. *(laughs)* I know. Come on. *(Coaxing JANEEN to join. She sings.)*
I WANT A PICKLE WITH A BONE IN IT....."
(to JANEEN) Come on.
I WANT A PICKLE WITH A ...."
(JANEEN softly joins in. She is awkward and less confident with her movements.)

JANEEN & LAVEER.
I WANT A PICKLE WITH A BONE IN IT. UNGH. UNGH.

LAVEER. *(to JANEEN)* You got to put more in it, Janeen.
(demonstrates)
UNGH. UNGH.
(The girls start the song up again. JANEEN puts more into her

singing and gyrations. She enjoys it.)
JANEEN & LAVEER.
I WANT A PICKLE WITH A BONE IN IT. UGH. UNGH.
(The girls laugh.)
LAVEER. I like that one.
JANEEN. It's nasty.
LAVEER. It's fun.
JANEEN. *(insisting)* It's nasty!
LAVEER. *(insisting)* It's fun! *(silence)* Hair time. *(She unbraids her hair.)* I want a real different style today.
JANEEN. What kind?
LAVEER. Different. Grown up, but different. And not like Miss Robinson's *(JANEEN begins to comb and style LAVEER's hair.)*
JANEEN. You know what I want to be when I grow up?
LAVEER. A princess.
JANEEN. A lady of leisure.
LAVEER. *(laughing)* Where'd you hear that one?
JANEEN. *(confused and embarrassed)* From Miss Thomas. I heard her talking with my mother.
LAVEER. You know what a lady of leisure does?
JANEEN. No. What? *(LAVEER looks around her environment and then whispers in JANEEN's ear. JANEEN is shocked.)* You lie! .... Who told you that?
LAVEER. Read it.
JANEEN. Where?
LAVEER. In a book.
JANEEN. What book?
LAVEER. The one my mother hides.

JANEEN. You lie.

LAVEER. Cross my heart. The bookcase next to the window. Besides, why should I lie? You learn a lot from reading those books.

JANEEN. Those are grown up books. You can't read all the words in those books.

LAVEER. That's what dictionaries are for.

JANEEN. What else do they say? They talk about sex?

LAVEER. *(nonchalantly)* Yep.

JANEEN. *(excited)* They do?

LAVEER. Yep.

JANEEN. I don't believe you.

LAVEER. I can prove it.

JANEEN. How?

LAVEER. *(Retrieves a book from her school bag, flips through pages, then reads.)* "He took me as I had always dreamed, tenderly, passionately...." *(She stops and looks at Janeen.)*

JANEEN. "Passionately....." Well, don't stop.

LAVEER. Like it huh? .....

JANEEN. *(embarrassed)* Laveer...... *(JANEEN quickly finishes LAVEER's hair and sits beside LAVEER and listens attentively.)*

LAVEER. "I knew I would let him. I would let him take me with the strength of his man. Allow him to move through the channel of my life giving waters and explode .... Oh .... to have him explode like the most violent of volcanoes. To have him erupt his passion ..... Consequences .... I have no concern for consequences. I care only for this now, for his touch, his lips, his loving. I am his. I am his to take me, take me as he so sees fit."

(LAVEER stops reading. She savors the words for a moment and then replaces the marker in the book and then buries the book once again in the book bag. She turns to JANEEN whose face is still marked with astonishment.)

JANEEN. Wow weee .... Did you hear that?

LAVEER. Nope. I read it.

JANEEN. How many times?

LAVEER. Four or five.

JANEEN. You read that five times?

LAVEER. *(touching her hair, approving)* Yep.

JANEEN. The whole book or just those pages?

LAVEER. The whole book.

JANEEN. It got any real nasty parts?

LAVEER. Yep. Want to take it home?

JANEEN. *(hesitant)* I'd like to..... *(LAVEER digs into her book bag.)* But....

LAVEER. *(replacing the book)* But what?

JANEEN. Well .....

LAVEER. Well what?

JANEEN. Suppose I get caught?

LAVEER. You won't get caught, unless you go around announcing it. *(placing her hands about her mouth and making a megaphone)* "I'm reading dirty books!"

JANEEN. Shuuuuu .....

LAVEER. Or you run around with guilt written all over your face. Or you get caught breathing too hard when you're suppose to be in bed sleeping.

JANEEN. You do that?

LAVEER. What?

JANEEN. Breathe hard.

LAVEER. Only on the real nasty parts.

JANEEN. Wow.
LAVEER. Won't you take it home and read it for yourself.
JANEEN. I can't.
LAVEER. Why?
JANEEN. I don't know ...... No back bone, don't have straight legs.
LAVEER. Oooooo I hate that expression of yours. Where'd you get it from anyway?
JANEEN. Grandpa.
LAVEER. You ought to give it back.
JANEEN. He says people who are afraid don't have back bone or straight legs.
LAVEER. That's a yyyulky way to think about yourself, you know. You ought to wrap up all your grandfather's sayings and give 'um back.
JANEEN. You're wierd. How do you think things like that?
LAVEER. I'm ahead of my time. I'm a nonconformist.
JANEEN. A nonconformist? Who told you that?
LAVEER. I read it, and after careful examination I decided that I am. It's what I want to be, besides a painter. I'm going to be a famous, famous painter. Anyway the two seem to go hand in hand.
JANEEN. What?
LAVEER. Nonconformist and painter. *(Runs her fingers over her new and unusual hair style.)* This feels great. *(referring to her hair)*
JANEEN. Your mother's going to kill you.
LAVEER. Nope. What she's gonna do is .... *(demon-*

strates) Grab her heart, back herself into a corner, look up at the ceiling and ask God what she did to deserve all of this, meaning me. Then.... after her speech.... *(She points her finger and shakes it at JANEEN, mimicking her mother.)* "Haven't I told you about...." And then she'll list them. She'll tell me to go upstairs and comb this mess out of my hair.

JANEEN. So why do it if you know she's going to yell and she's going to make you comb it out?

LAVEER. Why not? Besides it feels good.

JANEEN. My mother says going through life feeling things can get you in a lot of trouble.

LAVEER. And your mother's frustrated most of the time too.

JANEEN. She's not.

LAVEER. She is.

JANEEN. *(holding her ground)* She's not!

LAVEER. You told me so yourself.

JANEEN. I didn't.

LAVEER. You did.

JANEEN. When?

LAVEER. Last September. We were sitting on my back porch eating pomegranates. Remember?

JANEEN. *(remembering)* Well ....

LAVEER. Well hell ....

JANEEN. Laveer ..... Your mouth.

LAVEER. What about my mouth?

JANEEN. It's filthy.

LAVEER. So.

JANEEN. It's not ladylike.

LAVEER. But it's fun. Besides I'm not sure I want to be a lady.

JANEEN. Everybody should want to be a lady.

LAVEER. Not if we have to end up like our moms. Yelk! Too many 'I can'ts' or 'I shouldn'ts' for me.

JANEEN. They're respected.

LAVEER. So who cares about being respected? I want to be daring, risky. I want to ...

JANEEN. Be like Francine Willis.

LAVEER. Bet she has more fun than we do. And what's so great about being a virgin and never kissed? I want to kiss somebody. I want to stick my tongue in ..... *(thinks)* Darrel Rivers mouth and let him put his hands right here. *(Indicates her small breasts.)*

JANEEN. *(Shocked. Looks around the environment. Whispers.)* You don't mean that.

LAVEER. Yep.

JANEEN. Your tongue in his mouth?

LAVEER. Yep.

JANEEN. That's nasty. It's swapping spit.

LAVEER. It's French Kissing. Doris Day and Rock Hudson don't kiss the way real people kiss. Anyway, I think Darrel has cute lips.

JANEEN. You're going to get in trouble.

LAVEER. If you ask me most of life is gonna get you in trouble. Might as well have some fun. You gotta stop being a scardy cat.

JANEEN. I'm not.

LAVEER. You are.

JANEEN. Am not!

LAVEER. Are!

JANEEN. Well everybody can't be like you! Anyway, my father said, if it weren't for the weak there wouldn't be the strong.

LAVEER. Your father, your grandfather, your mother .... Sometimes you make me so mad with all the things you believe your family says.

JANEEN. They're older and wiser.

LAVEER. They're jerks.

JANEEN. They are not!

LAVEER. I don't mean to talk about your family, but.... They're too boxed in for me. Look, Janeen, you can't go around doing things 'cause somebody said this or that about it. You got to do what you want to do sometimes.

JANEEN. And get in trouble.

LAVEER. So you get in trouble.

JANEEN. And you get put on punishment.

LAVEER. So you get put on punishment. I stay on punishment, but I also have fun. *Sometimes* it's worth it. Besides, who gets hurt? Nobody.

JANEEN. If you kiss Darrel you might get pregnant.

LAVEER. I didn't say I was going to do it with him. I said I wanted to tongue kiss him. You think I'm crazy? I do it with Darrel and my daddy finds out .... He'd skin me alive and then swing me off the front porch. I ain't crazy.

JANEEN. I wish I could be like you.

LAVEER. You don't want to be like me. You want to be like you. Just do things you want to do. Okay?

JANEEN. How do you know so much about life?

LAVEER. I read dirty books.

JANEEN. But you're not afraid to do things.

LAVEER. That's 'cause I'm going to die when I'm twenty-one.

JANEEN. You are not.

LAVEER. I am. You see. I've decided I'm going to be an artist. That's because I'm ahead of my time. And I'm going to do everything, travel all over the world, have great lovers ... see all kinds of things and be famous, but ... I'm going to have to experience tragedy. Artists have to do that you know. So, I'm going to die at twenty-one.

JANEEN. Nobody knows when they're going to die.

LAVEER. I do.

JANEEN. You don't.

LAVEER. I do. But .... in the mean time. I am going to live, and be the best artist ever.

JANEEN. *(staring at LAVEER)* I wish we were real sisters, twins. Then I could be like you.

LAVEER. Janeen!! Will you stop that! It's okay being Janeen. 'Sides, how you gonna be my twin? You can't draw. And forget that lady of leisure. You don't have what it takes to be a lady of leisure.

JANEEN. Promise me you'll always be my best friend. Promise.

LAVEER. Promise.

JANEEN. I mean ..... mean it.

LAVEER. I do.

JANEEN. Really mean it.

LAVEER. *(frustrated)* I do.

JANEEN. You'll always be my best friend and my sister.

LAVEER. Promise.

JANEEN. And help me to have straight legs?

LAVEER. Janeen! ..... I promise.

JANEEN. Swap hair on it.

LAVEER. Jesus ..... Again?

JANEEN. Swap hair on it.

LAVEER. You're gonna make me bald with all this swapping. *(The two girls pull hair from one anothers head.)*

(The lights dim.)

Scene II

Sound. A song. It is sung in darkness by the voices of young female adults. It is a spoof on a traditional college alma mater.

WOMEN. *(singing)*
AND THROUGH THE THICK AND THIN
RACIAL WORDS AND SNARLING GRINS
WE WILL PERSEVERE UNTIL THE END
AND MAKE THEIR SMALL MINDS SPIN

WE ARE THE FIRST
WE ARE THE BEST
WE ARE THE ONES TO HOLD THE FINAL CONQUEST

AND IN THE END
THEY'LL LOOK BACK AND SAY
THOSE RAINBOW SIX
THEY WERE MORE THAN A CREDIT
THEY WERE MORE THAN EROTIC

THOSE RAINBOW SIX
WITH THEIR BRAINY BRAINS
THEY SURPASSED THE PAINS

THOSE RAINBOW SIX
A FEW PRANKS AND TRICKS
THOSE RAINBOW SIX

ACT I LONG TIME SINCE YESTERDAY 17

THOSE RAINBOW SIX
THOSE RAINBOW SIX
THEY WERE THE BEST.

(A twenty-seven year period has lapsed between the previous scene of the young girls and this. Lights rise on modern living room of a split level dwelling. A staircase and landing protrude over playing area. [This is JANEEN's domain.] There are bookcases laden with medical and educational books and a special section on erotica. A modern plush designer sectional sofa dominates the furnishings. It is accentuated with several throw pillows. A tall chrome floor lamp hovers over one section of the sofa. Other furnishings dressing the set should be quality items reflecting the upward mobile status of the inhabitants.

Enter LAVEER SWAN, attractive woman of thirty-eight. She is a professional painter/artist. LAVEER dangles a loose set of keys in hand. She is followed by ALISA MYERS-REYNOLDS, attractive woman of thirty-nine. She is the director of a pre-school program. ALISA wears glasses and walks with a stylish, quite feminine, walking cane. PANZI LEW McVAIN, THELMA CARLSON, and BABBS WILKERSON follow ALISA.

PANZI LEW McVAIN, extremely attractive woman of thirty-eight. She has a beautifully proportioned and shapely figure. She is a physical therapist.

THELMA CARLSON, less attractive than the other women. She is more the 'Plain Jane'. She wears little or no makeup and hides attractive eyes behind thick glasses. Her clothing is much darker than that worn by the other women. She is a medical doctor opening a new medical clinic.

BABBS WILKERSON, very fair, attractiveness attributed to makeup and the art of application. She is thirty-seven and the most fashion conscious of the women. She is an anchor person at a news station in Minneapolis, Minnesota.

All women wear suitable attire and colors reflecting the past funeral service. The women carry single stem flowers and/ or programs from the interment. PANZI and THELMA are most conservative in their dress, both wearing tailored suits or attire. LAVEER is the exception among the women. She wears an artsie, almost sensual, bright mint green and black dress. She is ladden in authentic and interesting jewelry, mostly gold, from her years of traveling. LAVEER also wears a huge black sun hat with veil which requires great distance between she and the others. With the veil drawn back, she wears the hat for a lengthy portion of this scene.

There is a tone of somber memory and grief as the women move into the environment.)

BABBS. *(studying the environment)* 'Dark Emptiness.'

ALISA. *(to BABBS)* What?

BABBS. A little something I once heard regarding life after death. *(She scans the room.)* 'Dark Emptiness.'

THELMA. Yes ... *(studying the environment)* This could keep Walter away. You know they say he hasn't stepped foot back in here since he found Janeen.

ALISA. Grief sometimes does that. *(LAVEER draws open the curtains. A flood of sunlight spills into the room.)*

BABBS. Now that's better. *(observing the environment)* Beautiful. One thing you could always say about Janeen, she had taste.

THELMA. That she did.

ALISA. *(before the library)* Fine collection.

BABBS. *(joining ALISA at the library)* And as usual everything in its place. *(reading book titles)* An education section. *(to ALISA)* Your area. *(continues reading titles)* Ah, Thelma.... Good old medicine. Must be Walter's section. *(continues reading titles)* And erotica. *(She turns to LAVEER as in playful accusation.)* I wonder who influenced this. *(She takes a book and flips through the pages.)*

THELMA. *(to ALISA)* So tell me about that leg of yours.

ALISA. Nothing much to tell. A tractor trailer jumped the median, caused a pile up of five cars on the inter-state and left me with my souvenir. *(Indicates her leg.)* Almost lost it, but for a lot of help from a good friend. *(Indicates PANZI.)*

BABBS. Oh ... Madame Panzi Lew McVain, therapist, to the rescue. Now tell me networking doesn't pay off.

PANZI. She was a good patient, a real worker. She could have lost complete use of that leg.

ALISA. So they told me. Anyway, I've resigned myself to the distinguished look of my customized cane.

THELMA. *(embracing ALISA while walking to the sofa)* We all have our crosses to bear.

ALISA. So we do. Besides, it wasn't all as bad as it

seems. During that dreadful cast-wearing stage ... *(to THELMA and PANZI)* You know the itching part right smack in the middle where the pencil and the ruler don't reach.... Lloyd and I discovered some nice kinky positions.

THELMA. Do tell.

BABBS. A noted reason why the Reynolds clan continues to grow.

ALISA. Well someone among the group has to perpetuate the growth of mankind.

BABBS. *(to the group of women)* Now is that a dig or is that a dig?

LAVEER. *(to ALISA)* How many is it now?

ALISA. Five.

LAVEER. Jesus.

BABBS. Jesus had nothing to do with it.

THELMA. How do you have time to run that pre-school of yours?

BABBS. Half of the students are hers. *(She laughs.)*

LAVEER. *(to ALISA)* You're not teaching anymore?

ALISA. Nope. Having the babies opened my eyes to the need for pre-school environments for the working mother.... So..... With a lot of help from Lloyd and a little help from the bank.... I've got my own school. *(PANZI and LAVEER have both taken positions on the exterior during the course of the dialogue between the women. THELMA, ALISA and BABBS are more central in their positions. Periodically PANZI and LAVEER's eyes meet from their opposite positions. It is obvious there is tension between them.)*

THELMA. *(to ALISA)* I admire that in you.

ALISA. What?

THELMA. You've got the best of both worlds.

ALISA. So what's stopping you? In fact, what's stopping all of you? As you know dear ladies, life will not stop and wait for you. You've got to get on in here and get your piece of this pie before the child bearing years are a thing of the past.

BABBS. Count me out. The thought of two a.m. feedings and diaper changes .... Ooooooo. *(She shrugs her shoulders and shakes.)* Reminds me of the time I was living in New York with this thigh-high poodle ..... *(She demonstrates the dog's height.)* Lady was her name. God, I was forever having to take that dog for a walk. Got rid of it as quick as I could. Can you see me doing that to a baby? .... *(to ALISA)* I leave the child bearing and rearing stage of life to you, with my compliments.

THELMA. *(to ALISA)* I'm not going to be quite as dramatic, but you'll excuse me if I do the mothering thing vicariously.

ALISA. Give me one good reason why.

THELMA. Well, some of us....

BABBS. *(to THELMA)* Don't you dare bring up that tired ass excuse from yesterday. If you do. I will personally strangle you with these two hands.

THELMA. Well you've got to admit, when God gave out beauty I was somewhere in line getting seconds on brains.

BABBS. You see that! That kind of thinking is not healthy. Oooo you make me so sick with that kind of thinking. I mean it. You are not ugly Thelma. I have seen ugly people in my day, and believe me you are not ugly. You could stand to fluff up some, but .... *(to the group)*

Have you seen her eyes? God gave Thelma the most beautiful pair of eyes with naturally long lashes ..... *(to THELMA)* If you'd just fluff up some, throw those ugly ass grandma Lulibelle glasses of yours in the garbage, invest in some contacts, make-up and a new wardrobe you'd be surprised what you'd find. God, if I didn't spend half my monies at the cosmetic counter I'd look like Miss Plain Jane myself. Cosmetics do do wonders, don't they? *(She flamboyently models and laughs. To THELMA.)* So .... Get your show on the road. *(crosses to THELMA)* You know I love you, but I hate, hate, hate it when you put yourself down. I really do. *(turning to the group)* Would anyone know the whereabouts of the bathroom?

LAVEER & PANZI. *(simultaniously)* It's off the hall, down the left and .... *(They stop. Silence. The two women stare at one another. A rising wave of tension permeates the room.)*

BABBS. *(to LAVEER)* Lavy, would you be so kind as to escort me? It's this cystitis again. Can't seem to break the cycle of reoccurance. I drink the cranberry juice, but ... stop the cystitis? *(BABBS and LAVEER exit. Silence.)*

PANZI. The nerve. I mean the gall of it all. What's she doing here?

ALISA. I think you call it mourning the death of a friend.

PANZI. Laveer was never Janeen's friend.

ALISA. That's a matter of opinion.

PANZI. You were always on Laveer's side.

ALISA. I beg your pardon. I was never on anyone's side. That feud was between you, Janeen and Lavy.

PANZI. And did you see how she strutted up to Walter

and asked for the keys to this house? Like she and Janeen had been bosom buddies.

THELMA. From the way the story goes, they used to be, remember? It hasn't been that long.

PANZI. Used to, as in past tense. I can't stand the bitch.

ALISA. Alright Panzi.

PANZI. Sashaying around with those keys like she was a friend to Janeen. I was Janeen's friend.

ALISA. So we all were. Is Thelma raising her blood pressure over those keys? Am I? What is with you, Panzi? Caaaaarist! Walter gave the keys to Lavi and that's that.

THELMA. *(to PANZI)* Had you considered the man is still in shock? Besides, I heard Mrs. Earl tell Lavy to get the keys from Walter and bring us over here. I'm sure there was no malicious thought intended.

ALISA. The girls go back to elementary school. What do you expect at a time like this? Who's thinking logically? Obviously you're not.

PANZI. *(fighting tears)* You don't understand. I was her friend. *(breaks)* I was ..... Me ..... They ignored me. The whole family.

ALISA. No one ignored you.

PANZI. I tell you, they did. *(fighting her emotions)* Not once did Walter ever come over to me. He didn't even respond to me when I offered my help with the funeral arrangements. I was Janeen's best friend, me, not that...

THELMA. But Panzi ... The three of them grew up together. People forget about quarrels and falling outs at times like this.

PANZI. I have stood by Janeen ever since graduation. Me. I was her maid of honor .... I .... Laveer wasn't ever invited to the wedding. *(fighting the tears)* They treated me like ..... I wasn't consulted about anything. *(ALISA crosses to PANZI to comfort her.)* Not even the flowers. I could have helped with the arrangements. But no .... Who did they contact? Who did they bring all the way up here from Mexico? .... That damn ..... bitch has always been in my fucking way!

ALISA. Calm down Panzi. I know how you feel.

PANZI. No you don't know how I feel! Neither one of you *know* how I feel.

(LAVEER and BABBS enter. Their voices can be heard offstage.)

BABBS. *(offstage)* I loved Mexico. It was one of those romantic ventures we used to read about in those romance books. You know, the kind we used to read under the sheets by flash light. Remember those? You know, erotica with a little taste. Anyway, Acapulco was a chapter straight out of one of those *nicer* kinds. Frank and I spent our honeymoon there. Too bad we couldn't have lived there, might have kept the romance going, but .... We came north, my rose-tinted glasses cleared, Frank changed into the bland, non-spirited, non-commital man of the seventies and my marriage went to putt.

THELMA. Where's he now?

BABBS. Frank? Who knows? Who cares? We got a quick one, two, three divorce in the Dominican Republic. And ... you won't believe, but ... We weren't through signing all the legal documents when Frank had visions of sugar plums in his head. The divorce formalities were finished at eleven. He was married to young Miss twenty-two-year-old Madilane What's Her Name at three p.m. There she was, a complete carbon copy of me, right down to her hair do. Twenty-two and I was thirty-four ... The child even flew down on the same plane as me. I remembered thinking I liked the dress she was wearing when she walked past me to the ladies room. It wasn't until after the divorce and Frank's new marriage that I realized that her dress was very similar to the dress he had bought me for my birthday a year before. I think I drank a case of brandy that evening all by myself. *(to THELMA)* No, I do not know where Frank is, and I could care less.

ALISA. *(Silence. To LAVEER.)* I've been hearing some good things about you and your art. You're in Mexico now aren't you?

LAVEER. San Miguel de Allende.

THELMA. There's an artist community down there, isn't it?

LAVEER. A few.

ALISA. Elizabeth Catlett still there?

LAVEER. Not is San Miguel, but she's still in Mexico.

THELMA. I've got to get down to Mexico.

LAVEER. You're always welcome.

ALISA. *(proud)* Lavy, our world traveler. How many countries is it now?

LAVEER. Jesus .... Don't make me count.

ALISA. Well, you always said you wanted to travel.

BABBS. And travel she did. You ought to have her tell you about this Egyptian who wanted her to be his.... *(to LAVEER)* What number wife was it? Third?

LAVEER. Third.

BABBS. And the Nigerian Prince or what ever he was ..... You ought to see the gold those two men had her dripping in. *(Crosses to LAVEER. She inspects LAVEER's hands and wrists.)* Ah yes .... She didn't pawn them.

ALISA. That's right, you and Lavy have kept in touch over the years.

BABBS. She better have. I would have killed her if she had forgotten me. This child lives a life straight out of the romance books. A man in Paris, one in Italy, two in South America, one on this island, four or five on that .....

THELMA. *(Laughs. To LAVEER.)* You'd better watch out for herpes.

LAVEER. Precisely why I'm down in San Miguel. One man, one quiet life and my paint brushes. It's safer.

BABBS. That'll last only until they find a cure for herpes. *(The group laughs. All except PANZI.)*

PANZI. Listen, would anyone care for something to drink?

ALISA. I could use one. Bourbon.

THELMA. Wine, white.

BABBS. To hell with the cystitis and the medication. I want a brandy snifter filled with about this much.... *(She indicates about two inches.)* of brandy. *(to THELMA)* And Doctor Thelma Carlson, don't you say one word about what I should or should not be drinking.

THELMA. If you want to kill yourself go right ahead and kill yourself. *(The room falls into weighted silence. THELMA exhales.)* I sure didn't mean for that to come out like that.

ALISA. One of us was bound to say it sooner or later.

BABBS. I can't believe she did it. Now me.... I have the potential for the dramatic, but Janeen .... suicide?.....

LAVEER. She was weak.

PANZI. And Miss Laveer Swann, pillar of strength, knows it all.

LAVEER. Janeen was weak.

PANZI. You think because you went to kindergarden, junior high, high school and college with her that makes you an authority on who and what Janeen was, well it doesn't. You know nothing about her. Nothing! And you know what? I resent you being here. I resent you standing there all high and mighty, dressed like you were going out for afternoon cocktails, standing there like you were God herself, voicing profundities of 'She was weak.' What do you know of anything?

ALISA. Please. Let's have a little peace, for Janeen's sake. Please.

PANZI. Peace? How do you have peace with her around? We're suppose to be in mourning and Miss Arteeeeeeest here takes center stage discussing the many men of her life.

BABBS. Wait a minute, I brought that up.

PANZI. *(Ignoring BABBS. To LAVEER:)* Who gives a good damn how many men you've screwed to get a couple of rings and a bracelet? Who gives a damn? If I had had my way you would not be here.

LAVEER. And if you had not *had* your way Janeen might still be alive.

PANZI. Meaning?

LAVEER. Don't push me Panzi. Just don't push me. I will tolerate just but so much of your shit. You log that into your brain. I tolerate you only because I loved Janeen. Only because I loved....

PANZI. Love?! Women like you don't know the first thing about love.

LAVEER. Like I said, don't push me or ... *(pause)* You back up off me Panzi.

ALISA. Panzi. Come. Let me help you with the drinks. *(PANZI resists.)* Come on Panzi. I could use a good stiff bourbon right about now and so could you.

PANZI. *(to LAVEER while exiting)* Bitch.

ALISA. *(to LAVEER)* Forget it Lavy, it's the day, the funeral. You know? What are you drinking?

LAVEER. Nothing.

ALISA. Lavy.... I'm not mad at you, you're not mad at me. So what are you drinking?

LAVEER. Brandy.

ALISA. Thank you.

LAVEER. You're welcome. *(The two women embrace. ALISA exits.)*

THELMA. *(silence)* Can I ask you a question Lavy?

LAVEER. If I were to say no would it stop you?

THELMA. No.

LAVEER. *(pause)* Well ....

THELMA. It's sort of tied into what's got Panzi in such a huff.

BABBS. If you ask me she's always in a huff when you put she and Lavy in the same room. It's like watching a cock fight.

LAVEER. Please Babbs, a cock I am not.

BABBS. Well you two fight like two cocks.

THELMA. It's about the keys.

LAVEER. What about the keys?

THELMA. She feels, because she was Janeen's closest friend, Walter should have given the keys to her instead of you.

BABBS. A bit juvenile, but ....

THELMA. What with you and Janeen having been on the outs for so long, and her being so close to her, she feels the family should have consulted her instead of you concerning the service.

LAVEER. And the question.

THELMA. It's been a good seventeen years since that flair up at graduation ....

LAVEER. And ....

THELMA. It does appear strange the family called on you instead of her.

LAVEER. Possibly.

THELMA. What's really going on?

LAVEER. Life. *(She crosses to the window.)*

THELMA. You're not going to answer are you?

LAVEER. You're very perceptive.

THELMA. *(releasing the subject)* Okay.

LAVEER. *(silence)* What is there to say, Thelma? She commited suicide. *(silence)* Some things are best left alone. You know?

THELMA. Okay.

LAVEER. Some things are best left just where they are.

(Silence. The lights begin to change. THELMA and BABBS freeze. Lights rise on the adult JANEEN EARL-TAYLOR, attractive woman of thirty-eight. She is located on upper protuding landing

with phone in hand. This area is JANEEN's spiritual and flashback domain. All subsequent JANEEN scenes are flashbacks.)

JANEEN. Lavy? .... *(She waits.)*

LAVEER. *(confused)* Yes, this is she.

JANEEN. Lavy, this is a voice out of your past. Janeen. *(silence)* Are you there?

LAVEER. Yes.

JANEEN. Please, don't hang up. You won't hang up will you?

LAVEER. No.

JANEEN. Good. I was afraid you would. I .... I got your number from your mother. Our mothers are still members of the 'Trees.'

LAVEER. I know.

JANEEN. Mother talked Walter and me into joining. Oh, I married Walter.

LAVEER. I know. Are you happy?

JANEEN. Boy, you still go straight to the point. Am I happy? ... I guess so. He's still fine as ever. Great lips. Still kisses good. I guess so.

LAVEER. Why'd you marry him?

JANEEN. Why? Why do most people get married? Besides, you know my parents and his parents sort of decided we'd be a couple back at our first Christmas party. Remember? We were about five .... Sort of like the old days back in history, right out of one of those books .... huh? *(no response)* You still there?

LAVEER. Umm hum.

JANEEN. Boy, this is good reception. I didn't think

I'd get good lines calling into Mexico. How's the weather?

LAVEER. Fine.

JANEEN. And your love life? Your mother says you've got a new beau, a sculptor.

LAVEER. Yes.

JANEEN. Older I hear.

LAVEER. Twelve years.

JANEEN. Perfect. For you I mean. For me .... I'd turn him into my father. You know me.

LAVEER. Janeen, I'm no longer mad with you. I no longer think you're a spineless twerp, so ... Relax and tell me why you've called.

JANEEN. You're not? I mean, still mad?

LAVEER. Jesus ... You know how many years ago that was?

JANEEN. Long time. I was wrong you know. And sometimes I am a spineless twerp.

LAVEER. Maybe not quite a spineless twerp.

JANEEN. Sometimes. I don't want to be, but ... Decisions and me ... Never quite my forte. Seems sort of silly now, looking back on the fight.

LAVEER. We were younger.

JANEEN. I guess I felt you abandoned me, reneged on your promise.

LAVEER. What promise?

JANEEN. You promised you'd always be my friend.

LAVEER. I've never stopped being your friend.

JANEEN. But you said ...

LAVEER. I said I would not befriend Panzi and you ought to grow up.

JANEEN. Yeah .... I guess I still do. It's just that ... I didn't know how to have the two of you in my life at the same time. It was so hard. Always so much friction. I was always in the middle.

LAVEER. That's a long time ago, let's bury it, okay?

JANEEN. *(relieved)* Okay ..... Lavy?

LAVEER. Humm?

JANEEN. We still sisters?

LAVEER. *(laughs)* You're still such a little girl ..... Yes Janeen. Now, why'd you call?

JANEEN. Daddy died.

LAVEER. I'm sorry. When?

JANEEN. Last night. I ..... I don't know what to do. I mean, everything seems to be falling apart, giving way....

LAVEER. Where's Walter?

JANEEN. He's on a lecture circuit, recruiting students into his med. school. He wants to come home, but I told him to stay. He won't of course, but ... Mother's handling everything in grand fashion. The 'trees' are helping out as usual and .... Can you come? I'd like for you to be here. Would you come?

LAVEER. You sure you want this?

JANEEN. Oh yes. Please. Daddy would have wanted you to be here.

LAVEER. And what does Janeen want?

JANEEN. Janeen needs her friend. I still have your hair.

LAVEER. *(laughs)* You lie.

JANEEN. Truth. I do. It's in a little antique box. You won't believe how many strands of your hair I have.

LAVEER. Please don't tell me. My scalp aches at the mere thought. *(pause)* Janeen. One more question. Panzi. Where's Panzi?

JANEEN. She's on vacation in Switzerland.

LAVEER. *(understanding)* I see.

JANEEN. *(quickly)* No, it's not like you think. I could have called her. I mean, I just talked to her three days ago. I have her number there. She would come .... but ... I want you here .... Do you hear me Lavy?

LAVEER. Yes.

JANEEN. It is easier with her there. I mean, I don't feel like I have to take sides. Will you come?

LAVEER. I'll take the first flight out.

JANEEN. *(surprised)* You will? *(excited)* Oh good. I'll pick you up at the airport. Then we can stop off for an Italian hoagie and gorge ourselves while you tell me first hand the news I've been reading on your work. *(pause)* Lavy ..... thanks .... I love you.

(The lights dim on JANEEN. The lighting shifts back to that of the previous scene.)

BABBS. *(to LAVEER)* You alright?

LAVEER. Fine. *(insistingly)* Fine.

BABBS. Okay. *(to THELMA)* Our own doctor in the family. *(to LAVEER)* And she's opening her own clinic. She's moved right along since the grand old days? Yes?

LAVEER. *(to THELMA)* Your own clinic?

THELMA. I have a couple of partners. Nothing special, just a little something for the community.

BABBS. Note the tone of modesty. *(to THELMA)* I'm elated for your progress, but I wish you'd gone into gynocology. If I get cystitis one more time.

THELMA. Could be your diet.

LAVEER. Have you ever seen what her diet consists of? Pepsi's, Coke's and brandy. She doesn't know what water is.

BABBS. Water's nasty.

THELMA. Water does not have a taste.

BABBS. It tastes like chloride.

THELMA. Okay, don't check your diet. Just lay off the sodas, the booze and the heavy love making. Try a more gentle position.

BABBS. Round about this moment I'd love to try any position. You know the last time I had some?

LAVEER. *(laughs)* Last night.

BABBS. Nine months .... *(thinks)* Three weeks ... No ... Let me not lie. *(She opens her bag, retrieves her appointment book and checks.)* Three and a half weeks and about .... *(Checks her watch.)* thirteen hours. November the fifteenth to be exact. His name was Sean Meers, a bore, wealthy, couldn't kiss and was less than desirable in the sack. A real Wall Streeter. Spent most of his time running his fingers through my hair and questioning the amount of caucasian blood in my veins. *(Disgusted she closes the book and drops it back into her bag.)* Enough to make a person consider hara-kiri. *(She stops herself.)* Not quite appropriate huh? *(pause)* I wonder where they went to get those drinks.

THELMA. *(silence)* Hard to believe she did it.

BABBS. Suicide and me, yes ... Janeen .... *(She shakes her head.)*

LAVEER. What do you mean you 'yes'?

(Enter ALISA and PANZI with the drinks and a tray of light hors d'oeuvres.)

BABBS. I tried. *(to ALISA and PANZI)* Ah .... Finally. *(Crosses to them.)* And munchies.... *(She picks from the tray.)* Caviar? Like I said, Janeen always did have taste. *(She takes her drink.)*
LAVEER. *(to BABBS)* What do you mean you tried?
BABBS. I tried.
LAVEER. When?
BABBS. Two weeks ago.
THELMA. You're putting us on.
ALISA. Putting us on about what?
BABBS. Suicide.
ALISA. What is happening with us?
BABBS. I don't know about us, but .... I took myself a sensual bath, in a tub of perfumed bubbles. Put on my sexiest gown. Fluffed up my face. Turned on the oven. Blew out the pilot. Reclined my body on my bed in a manner befitting Cleo herself and waited .... Unfortunately my neighbor's car alarm went off for the sixth time that week. The ringing gave me a headache, the gas was giving me a headache so ... The rest is history. I opened the windows, got dressed, went out for some fresh air and much to my chagrin am very much alive.
THELMA. Why?
BABBS. Why am I alive or why did I do it? *(Laughs. Gulps down her brandy.)* Because .... *(to PANZI)* Would it be too

much to request a refill?

PANZI. You sure you don't want a coke or...

BABBS. I'd like another .... *(Indicates the glass.)* Please. *(PANZI takes the glass and exits. BABBS calls to PANZI.)* It might be easier on your legs if you just brought the bottle back with you. *(to the group)* Please. Shocked stares and gapping mouths do not appeal such an illustrious group.

LAVEER. What are you doing to yourself, Babbs?

BABBS. *(chuckles)* I don't know. Engrossed in self pity.

THELMA. Pity ..... For God's sake why?

BABBS. Little things ..... Big things .... I guess it's a matter of perspective.

ALISA. And what's your perspective?

BABBS. Mine? .... Babbs tried to commit suicide. Janeen committed suicide and... God, what I'd give to be back in Steven's Hall, blanketed by the safety of college life.... *(to THELMA)* You used to tell me I was lucky to have this hair and these eyes. Remember? Well.... it's not so lucky. Sometimes, I look in the mirror and I think all of this .... *(Indicates her being.)* a curse. It's so middle of the road, not connected to anything, close enough to everything.... It shits. Life shits. *(pause)* I've been doing a little assessment thing on my life. You know what I found? All the opportunities, all the fine things I get out of life ... These eyes, this hair, this coloring .... *(She indicates.)* the calling card. A noted reason I hold the anchor spot in Minneapolis. It's called not being offensive to the eye.

THELMA. You don't believe that.

BABBS. The hell I don't.

LAVEER. We're suppose to believe it has nothing to do with your skills?

BABBS. In Minneapolis? I'm a safe route. White men who want a black woman.... Safe. *(She pats her chest.)* Black men who want a white woman...... Safe. *(She pats her chest.)* Corporations who have to fill a quota .... Safe.

(Enter PANZI with BABB's brandy snifter and a full brandy decanter.)

BABBS. *(to PANZI)* Thought you got lost. *(taking the brandy snifter)* Thank you. *(drinks)* Where was I?

PANZI. I hope off the subject of suicide.

BABBS. *(to PANZI)* And I love you too, darling. *(to the group of women)* Did I tell you Frank married a woman who looked just like me?

LAVEER. Yes.

BABBS. Tells you where his head was, still is for that matter. Wonder why men are like that?

ALISA. Now don't go lumping all men into that basket.

BABBS. Okay. You're right. I'm wrong. Ninty-nine percent. *(to ALISA)* That alright with you? *(to the group)* You know what I'd like? .... Clarles Bishop. He was thirteen and I was twelve. He wore thick coke bottle glasses, was deep dark chocolate brown and loved the hell of Babbs Wilkerson just because he thought I was nice. Sure wish I knew where he was today.

PANZI. You know what I wish? I wish you would all respect this day for what it is.

ALISA. Just what is this day?
PANZI. Oh cute.
ALISA. It wasn't meant to be cute. I'd like to know. What do you expect out of us?
PANZI. A class reunion this isn't.
ALISA. So a class reunion it isn't, now what? What are we suppose to do? Sit around in a circle, rock back and forth, cry out 'wos'?...
THELMA. I come from a family who believes in rejoicing at a death.
PANZI. If you call Miss Drunk here .... *(Indicates BABBS.)* a sample of rejoicing at a death ..... Do excuse me, I've got a phone call to make. *(Exits in a huff.)*
BABBS. *(to exiting PANZI)* Well la di da to you, Miss Thing. *(She sits.)*
THELMA. I'm for some fresh air. *(Rises and opens the front door.)*
ALISA. Janeen's death really has her in a tizzy.
LAVEER. It ought to.
THELMA. She did have one point.
BABBS. What?
THELMA. The way we've been going on, you'd think we had nothing to be thankful for.
ALISA. I beg your pardon. I've got a man who's hooked on my good loving, children I adore, good health, a good life and no regrets....
LAVEER. I have no complaints.
BABBS. Well ....
ALISA. *(to BABBS)* You're problem is you don't know how to take life by the horns and use it. You make life too complicated. You have assets, use them. A man sees you

for something other than you are .... use him until the one with some sense comes along. And prepare yourself for reality. The one with some sense may never come along.

THELMA. God forbid.

ALISA. *(to BABBS)* If he doesn't what are you going to do? Stick your head in the oven? All this talk about suicide and depression .... What did it get Janeen. A beautiful woman down the drain ... Why? Life promises you nothing. No guarantees. Nothing. We each have to do the best with what we get.

THELMA. And some of us should have been as lucky.

BABBS. *(to THELMA)* Alright. That's it. I've had it with you and that pisspoor attitude you have about yourself. *(Crosses to THELMA.)* Sit down.

THELMA. What are you talking about?

BABBS. I'm talking about you. Sit. How you ever made it through the sixties and missed the 'Black is Beautiful' spirit is beyond me. Sit. *(She pushes THELMA into the chair.)* Today Doctor Thelma Carlson, you're gonna get a glimpse of what you have. Take off those glasses. *(BABBS retrieves a make-up kit from her rather large, stylish hand bag.)*

THELMA. *(to BABBS)* And what, may I ask, are you about to do?

BABBS. Appease me.

THELMA. Appease you? *(LAVEER and ALISA laugh.)*

BABBS. Appease me. I've been dying to do this for years. *(studying THELMA's face)* You might find you even like the end result.

THELMA. Babbs, don't waste your ....

BABBS. Don't worry about what I waste. Just keep still, sit back and let the master do her thing.

LAVEER. *(to THELMA)* Why don't you just enjoy the ride?

ALISA. You must admit, Babbs has taken an abrupt upswing of spirit. *(observing BABBS with the make-up)* Puts you in the mind of the time Janeen had her making up Lavy's face for that mock funeral.

THELMA. Do Jesus.

ALISA. Janeen, convinced Lavy was going to die at twenty-one.

LAVEER. *(laughs)* I was.

BABBS. Sure you were.

ALISA. I can still see the three of them, Janeen, Lavy and Panzi, coming out of that small-town fashion shop with that bright red dress.

THELMA. Bright Chinese orange red.

BABBS. Janeen rattling on about everyone getting everything just right. Panzi mumbling all the way to the bus stop about how ridiculous the whole thing was.

LAVEER. I have you to know it was not ridiculous.

BABBS. Tell that to Panzi.

LAVEER. I'd rather not.

ALISA. *(reminising)* Lord, that loud red dress?

LAVEER. I liked red in those days.

BABBS. *(Steps back to get a better look at her make-up work on THELMA. To THELMA.)* You're going to love this when I'm through.

ALISA. *(Crosses to THELMA, gives an approving nod. To LAVEER.)* What was the name of that morbid poem you used to recite?

LAVEER. Emily Dickinson's "My Life Closed Twice Before It's Close" is not a morbid poem.

BABBS. You repeated it a thousand times the week before the funeral.

THELMA. That was the best thing out of the whole shabang, the funeral. Janeen's orchestration of Laveer laying in state in the dorm lounge ....

ALISA. For three whole hours. God.... The entire campus marching around you .... *(Indicates LAVEER.)* laying there, hands clasped over your breast and that fire engine red dress .....

LAVEER. Chinese red.

ALISA. Whatever.

THELMA. And Panzi giving that eulogy.

LAVEER. Horrendously ....

ALISA. Ah ah ah .... Now you, Janeen and Panzi were like three little peas in a pod in those days.

LAVEER. Panzi and I were never anything in *those days.*

ALISA. Now Lavy ....

THELMA. *(to LAVEER)* It took me months to get used to calling you Lavy instead of Laveer. Janeen correcting everyone, all the time saying .....

GROUP. *(simultaneously)* "Lavy" .....

BABBS. I'll never forget it. February the twenty-fifth.

ALISA. *(correcting)* A snowy February the twenty-fifth.

THELMA. Quite snowy .....

BABBS. Janeen waved her hands over the reclining Madame Swan .... *(Waves her hand over THELMA's head.)*

ALISA. Wait .... *(Demonstrates over the sofa.)* "Rise Lavy.

Rise Lavy. Laveer has gone to rest, but rise to life Lavy.... Venture no longer in darkness. Step from ...." And I just loved this line .... "Step from beyond the veil ...."

THELMA. Oh God, that's when Panzi waved this white lace thing they had dyed this grotesque grey over Lavy's body and ...

ALISA. "Rise Lavy ... We need you Lavy. We love you Lavy. Life is here lavy ....." And the child rose.

BABBS. Pure theatre. Janeen missed her calling.

(ALISA, THELMA and BABBS laugh.)

LAVEER. I have you to know we got an 'A' in drama for that event of which you are now making mockery.

ALISA. *(to LAVEER)* So much for you dying at twenty-one.

LAVEER. I died didn't I?

ALISA. And you rose, but don't expect me to gather the multitude an follow you down into Mexico ..... Funny, Janeen was the one who thought we were all going to live forever. I'd have never thought she'd ...

BABBS. She was a light bulb wasn't she?

LAVEER. On the days she believed in herself, yes.

THELMA. Always good for a laugh.

(Enter PANZI. She crosses to her bag and retrieves a cigarette.)

ALISA. Yeah, you could always count on Janeen's theatrics to pull you out of a slump.

BABBS. Into everything. *(to LAVEER)* I'm glad you and Janeen got things straightened out before .....

THELMA. To tell you the truth, I was really hurt when

the three of you fell out on graduation day. I mean, graduation day .... Lord what a time to do a thing like that.

BABBS. Well things have improved a bit over the years. Now if you and Panzi could just patch things up I'd feel even better.

ALISA. I'll second that. I've never been one who cared too much for friction, except that kind of friction me and Lloyd make beneath the sheets.

THELMA. Do tell.

BABBS. She always did have sex on the brain. *(Refers to ALISHA.)*

ALISA. I did not. I do now, but then ... I did not.

LAVEER. Ha. As I recall there was a night we all stayed over your room ....

BABBS. The night we had that freak snow storm.

LAVEER. The precise night. Janeen's feet got cold and you told ....

ALISA. Oh no .... Please don't bring that up.

LAVEER. *(to ALISA)* You told Janeen to get a pair of socks out of your drawer and she found a pack of ...

THELMA. Prophylactics. And Alisa had to spend the entire night telling Janeen step by step what it was like to have sex.

LAVEER. I mean, step by step. Alisa was the only one out of the six of us who wasn't a virgin.

PANZI. Oh, you were not a virgin Laveer.

LAVEER. I was.

PANZI. Why lie?

LAVEER. Why should I lie? I was a virgin.

PANZI. You were not a virgin.

LAVEER. *(tension building)* How are you going to tell me what I wasn't?

PANZI. Because I know.

LAVEER. Would it be too much to ask how? You inspect me with your little finger while I was sleeping or something?

ALISA. Okay you two ....

BABBS. I told you you can't have the two in one space without ...

LAVEER. Telling me what I wasn't.

PANZI. You weren't.

ALISA. Can't you two be in the same room without...?

LAVEER & PANZI. *(simultaneously)* No.

LAVEER. On that we do agree.

BABBS. Well, that's progress.

LAVEER. I need a refill. *(Refers to her glass.)* Anyone care to replenish their goblet?

BABBS. *(Extends her glass. To THELMA.)* And don't you say a word.

THELMA. Who's saying anything. I have a toll-free number to AA, remind me to give it to you.

BABBS. *(to LAVEER)* I'll take a refill.

ALISA. I could use another one.

LAVEER. Why don't I just bring back the bottles, then we can all use that toll-free number to AA. *(LAVEER exits. Silence.)*

ALISA. *(to PANZI)* I thought you were going to try to be civil.

PANZI. I am being civil.

BABBS. What is it between you two anyway?

PANZI. It's simple .... I can't stand the ....
BABBS. 'Bitch.' We know, the question is why?
PANZI. I don't like her type.
ALISA. Oh God, we're back to graduation day again.
BABBS. Do you know how many years ago that was?
THELMA. Too many for all this ruckus.
PANZI. Look, Laveer is a .... a mold of a type, and they're all the same ... Self centered, preoccupied in their beauty, their acquisitions, conquest and a lot too little concern for other's needs and feelings..... Janeen needed a friend who was genuinely concerned about her.
BABBS. Panzi Lew McVain.
PANZI. Time proved who her friend was.
BABBS. With a little help.
PANZI. Like I said, time and actions proved who Janeen's friend was. *(BABBS turns her attention to the cosmetic make-over of THELMA.)*
THELMA. Panzi.... How are you and that chess game of yours doing?
PANZI. My game? .... *(with light humor)* Superb as usual.
THELMA. *(referring to PANZI)* A little short on modesty, isn't she?
ALISA. *(laughs)* What do you expect from the woman who held the northeastern championship among the women's colleges? She's moved from those minor victories to the chessboard tournaments of Europe.
THELMA. Do tell. Well now, tell me our class didn't graduate and become the 'Who's Who' of this world? *(She laughs. To PANZI.)* Let me be the first among the ladies here to say I am quite proud of you.

PANZI. Thanks.

THELMA. But how you manage to work those tournaments into your hospital routine is beyond me. I'm lucky if I can make time to have a full-course dinner.

PANZI. That's because the therapy world is a lot different than your doctor world. Besides, every now and then I luck up on a patient who has a good game. Keeps my game sharp.

ALISA. I say bravo to anyone who can deal with that game.

BABBS. Too long and arduous for me.

THELMA. Never could quite handle it.

PANZI. *(lighting a cigarette)* It's all about skill, strategy and waiting out your opponent.

BABBS. Like I said, too long and arduous for me.

ALISA. It does go on forever, and without the benefits of Monopoly, no 'get out of jail free' cards, no buying up Park Place, Boardwalk ....

BABBS. *(to THELMA)* See what having babies does to you. *(referring to ALISA)*

ALISA. I beg your pardon, I've been playing Monopoly since I was a kid. You can learn a lot from Monopoly.

PANZI. You can learn a lot from chess.

ALISA. Chess lacks pazazz, color. It's gray. Like battlefields. A little move here. A little move there. Wait. Move. Wait. Think. Wait... I like spontaneity. Jump on in there and do it kind of spontaneity.

BABBS. Oh yeah, that we know.

THELMA. Don't we? *(to ALISA)* Eloping with Lloyd the way you did, without as much as a hint.

PANZI. Her chess game indicated she was capable of

doing that.

BABBS. How?

PANZI. She plays chess the way she lives her life.

ALISA. Oh God ..... please .... I play chess terribly.

PANZI. You're spontaneous, like you said. You're also lucky.

BABBS. *(to ALISA)* I think that's a dig back to the day you beat her at her own game.

PANZI. It was not, but she is lucky. How did she obtain her real estate portfolio? .... A dollar bill, a federal government housing program and what does she own today? .... Two apartment buildings.

ALISA. They're only two-story, eight apartment dwellings.

PANZI. And five houses on the top of Tioga Street. The neighbors call the area 'Reynolds Landing.' *(THELMA and BABBS laugh.)*

BABBS. 'Reynolds Landing'? ..... You can start your own night-time serial.

PANZI. And all from a dollar.

THELMA. Do tell.

PANZI. From the way she told me the story, she woke up one morning, glanced through the paper, saw an article on the government's new home-buying program and the rest is history.... Now is that spontaneity and luck or is it spontaneity and luck?

ALISA. *(Reflects on the phrase.)* Spontaneity and luck ..... Always amazes me how other people see things. Distance does that. *(Crosses to the window.)* Luck.... *(Turns to PANZI.)* I was about .... ten, my sister Joyce nine, Raymond fourteen, when our parents looked into our faces, looked around the room; the small kitchen, the livingroom with second-hand furniture, the house and family who'd gotten too much for them.... They made a decision to leave. *(BABBS sits.)* Just like that .... Leave. And they did. They placed a box of Cherios and Kellogg's Corn Flakes on the table, a half gallon of milk we'd just gotten from the Borden's milk man and left. Never came back. We waited, Raymond, Joyce and I .... We waited, but they never .... Raymond called a family meeting over the Monopoly game we'd started to pass the time. The topic, our next move. Another pang of reality after hopeless periodical peeks at the clock and front door. Raymond said, after seven long days of waiting and seven longer nights ... He said we were going to keep the family together. And we did.

THELMA. Dear God.

ALISA. Throughout the *whole* summer, until the fall, until school, nosy neighbors and teachers had the welfare agency at our door.... We were placed in separate foster homes .... *(to THELMA)* Separate new families .... *(to PANZI)* Until that lucky morning I put a dollar bill on a piece of real estate and put together what the neighbors call 'Reynolds Landing.' Maybe it should be called 'Meyers-Reynolds Landing' 'cause I reunited Joyce and Raymond ... and that's all of us up there .... All of us. *(silence)* So much for 'luck.'

PANZI. You know, if I had known I wouldn't have....

ALISA. Why should you? Why should any of you? All of you coming from respectable families. What was I suppose to do? Announce I had dogs for parents? No, not dogs, turtles ... Turtle mothers drop their eggs and then walk away. Was I suppose to tell you that? No. I let you believe what you wanted to believe. In the long run it was better for everyone. I hated my parents less and got on with living and learning; you do the best you can with what you get. *(PANZI lights another cigarette. ALISA stands before THELMA and studies THELMA's transformation. The make-up and new hair style have brought out her hidden attractiveness.)* Well would you take a look at our lady doctor?

THELMA. What?

BABBS. Well get up and take a look. *(THELMA rises and crosses to the mirror.)*

PANZI. *(approvingly)* Real nice.

THELMA. *(excited)* Really?

BABBS. Will you hurry up and look in that mirror?! *(BABBS follows THELMA to the mirror. BABBS stares between the mirror and THELMA's face to read her reaction. THELMA is pleasantly surprised. THELMA stares at herself. Silence. To THELMA.)* Well ....

THELMA. *(staring at her reflection)* I um.

BABBS. Articulate.

THELMA. Alisa .... Would you pass me my glasses?

BABBS. Oh please Thelma. Not those things. What you've got to do is get yourself some contacts.

THELMA. What I've got to do is see .... *(She holds her glasses up to her eyes to get a clearer view. She does not put the glasses on, but holds them up to see through the lenses. To BABBS.)* What did you do?

BABBS. You like?

THELMA. *(Tickled. Pleased.)* Like? ....

(Enter LAVEER with a tray holding the bottles of wine and spirits.)

LAVEER. I just spoke with my mother and the Trees are sending over something to eat..... *(Surprised by THELMA's transformation.)* Thelma?
BABBS. Our very own.
ALISA. Beautiful, yes?
THELMA. Can you believe?
BABBS. Now, if she'd get herself a pair of contact lenses she can show off those lashes.
THELMA. First chance I get. *(She embraces BABBS.)*
BABBS. That a promise?
THELMA. Um humm... Thank you. Now can I hire you to do this on a daily basis?
BABBS. *(to the group)* Now see that? .... Taking advantage of me already. *(to THELMA)* You may now look like a Nubian Queen, but don't let your head swell too big. *(The women laugh and refreshen their drinks, all but PANZI. PANZI crosses to the window.)*
ALISA. *(Crosses to PANZI.)* How are you doing?
PANZI. I should be asking you that. I'm sorry about earlier. I had no idea.
ALISA. That was a long time ago. But I am worried about you. You're okay?
PANZI. Yeah ... You know, it wasn't more than two months ago that we were sitting here in this room laughing, Janeen and me. Watching one of those Lou and Costello reruns. Janeen laughing that laugh only she could laugh.

(sound: JANEEN's vibrant laughter)

PANZI. She had such a great laugh.

ALISA. That she did. Puts me in the mind of our first year together. Most of us were in Blylor Hall .... You, Janeen and Lavy getting yourselves in this thing or the other. Janeen always laughing ....

THELMA. Like the time Fat Lucy tried to climb out the window on those blankets to see that acne-faced towny boy ...

BABBS. Oh God .... *(laughs)* Janeen hanging out her window watching Lucy screaming: "You're going to fall on your behind."

THELMA. No. You've got to say it the way she used to say it, in that little-girl, proper voice of hers.

ALISA. *(Mimics JANEEN.)* "You're going to fall on your behind."

PANZI. *(laughs)* And she started that laugh of hers.

ALISA. You mean that whoop. God, can you hear it?

THELMA. Hear it? Can't you just see Lucy hanging on for dear life on those blankets? All two hundred pounds of Lucy hanging out of the second-story window of Blylor Hall.

BABBS. And when Janeen said ....

LAVEER. *(a perfect imitation of JANEEN's voice)* "If you fall I'm going to scream. I mean it Lucy. If that blanket rips and you fall, I'm going to laugh at you ....." *(The women laugh violently. Then the laughter stops. They stare at LAVEER.)*

ALISA. *(to LAVEER)* If you didn't just sound like Janeen

.... Just like her.

THELMA. Just like her. *(PANZI is not impressed.)*

BABBS. *(to LAVEER)* You might be able to imitate her speaking voice, but that laugh ..... Nobody, but nobody could do that but her ..... *(She summons up the laughter again.)* 'Cause when Lucy fell ..... When that blanket ripped and big Fat Lucy hit those bushes, bounced up and sprawled herself out on that pavement ....

THELMA. Janeen let out that ......

ALISA. Whoop of hers.

THELMA. And all hell broke loose.

ALISA. Didn't it?

BABBS. I thought the child had killed herself. I mean, Lucy was laying out there all sprawled out like a whale beached up on the sand and ...

LAVEER. Janeen laughed so hard she peed on herself.

THELMA. She wasn't the only one. *(She points to ALISA.)*

ALISA. I didn't.

THELMA. Tell the truth.

ALISA. Well .... shit. Did you see Lucy? One leg over here .... *(demonstrates)* The other one hidden somewhere under that twenty tons of lard she carried around .....

THELMA. Her mouth all hung open like ..... *(demonstrates)*

BABBS. And that towny boy standing over her, staring down at her like he was crazed.

THELMA. The man was in shock. I mean how many times do you get to see Dumbo do her flying act and her ears fail?

BABBS. And fail they did, 'cause Lucy just bounced ..... I mean the girl just bounced off the bushes and splashed......

ALISA. You know.... Whenever I get a little low, when my spirits drop .... I think on Fat Lucy hanging onto those blankets, Janeen hanging out of that window....

PANZI. And that laugh.

ALISA. All I have to do is do an instant replay on that and ..... depression gets a back seat on the back burner.

LAVEER. Sometimes she could make me so mad, but .... When Janeen laughed.

ALISA. When she let out that whoop ......

THELMA. Hard to believe anyone who had that much life in her could ....

PANZI. I miss her. I really do.

(Lights dim.)

ACT II
Scene I

Lights rise on BABBS as she enters singing off key and with a slight variation on the melody.

BABBS. *(singing)*
SAVE ME. MISS YOUR LOVIN' ARMS.
YOU CAN SAVE ME. I BEEN CAPTURED....
(She refills her glass and drinks.)

(Enter ALISA, unnoticed. She observes BABBS' actions.)

BABBS. *(singing)*
SAVE ME. MISS YOUR LOVIN' ARMS.
YOU CAN SAVE ME. I BEEN CAPTURED
BY YOUR....
BY YOUR....
BY YOUR....
Shit! How'd those lyrics go? *(She drinks then continues singing.)*
BY YOUR CHARMS. COME ON. SAVE ME.
DON'T KNOW WHAT TO DO....
'CAUSE I'M.....
ALISA. It might help if you had the right melody and sang it in the right key.
BABBS. All of us were not blessed with melodic voices. Besides, I've been told singing is good for the soul. My soul likes to sing. *(ALISA stares at BABBS and the brandy snifter. To ALISA.)* Yes?

ALISA. What?
BABBS. What's wrong?
ALISA. Why do you ask that?
BABBS. You're giving me one of those motherly, concerned looks.
ALISA. Moi?
BABBS. Yes you.
ALISA. Well, it wasn't my intention to give the impression....
BABBS. You're not spying on me are you?
ALISA. Spying? .... Why should I be spying.....?
BABBS. You seemed quite comfortable in there.
ALISA. I could say the same of you. *(BABBS stares at ALISA. ALISA stares at BABBS.)*
BABBS. Alisa, I am simply trying to remember the lyrics to this song Janeen used to sing. *(ALISA nods.)* Panzi said it was a Supreme's song, I know better. *(BABBS drinks down the contents of her glass. ALISA stares at her.)* Alisa! Will you stop that?!
ALISA. What? What am I doing?
BABBS. Okay, alright. To allay any mounting fears or growing doubts .... I came in here simply to retrieve my glass. This glass. *(She indicates the snifter.)* A very elegant and beautiful brandy snifter, I might add, a tribute to Janeen's impeccable taste. *(She refills the brandy snifter.)* You could say I've grown attached to its touch.
ALISA. I see.
BABBS. *(Turns to ALISA.)* What do you see Alisa?
ALISA. You've grown attached to its touch. *(ALISA and BABBS fix their eyes on one another.)*
BABBS. Sometimes you see too much.

(LAVEER enters.)

BABBS. *(to LAVEER)* Got a little too crowded in there for you?

LAVEER. You could say the air's a bit fresher out here.

BABBS. It was on the verge of getting a little too crowded in here as well. *(She smiles, crosses to ALISA and then embraces her. To ALISA.)* But I love you anyway. *(to LAVEER)* You must tell your mother's club .... What's the name of that group again?

LAVEER. The 'Trees'.

BABBS. Right. Well, relay a great big 'thank you' for such a lovely meal.

ALISA. Ditto.

BABBS. It's scandalous anyone can fry a chicken the way that bird turned out. What's the name of your mother's club again?

LAVEER. *(correcting)* The correct term is .... 'Social and cultural enrichment organization'.

BABBS. Oh ... Excuse me.

ALISA. *(to LAVEER)* Do I sense a bit of cynicism?

LAVEER. *(cynically)* Cynicism, for a group whose social morals determine the rising and setting of the sun? Why should you sense a bit of cynicism?

BABBS. *(to ALISA)* Looks like you popped the cork on the wrong bottle.

LAVEER. The 'Trees' they're .... ticks. Old, powerful, domineering, meddlesome and let us not forget, benevolent and caring ticks.

BABBS. Who also know how to fry chicken.

LAVEER. Blood sucking ticks who dictate what you can and can not do, when you should or should not do, to whom you should or should not do or marry. They're a

ACT II LONG TIME SINCE YESTERDAY 57

nasty little batch of mothers and fathers who rule lives. My parents, Janeen's parents, Walter's parents.... A dangerous select group of 'decent' and I do stress the word 'decent' family-oriented professionals who promise success. See to success making you a doctor, lawyer, judge, wife of a doctor, lawyer, judge ....

BABBS. Sounds reminiscent of my family clan.

LAVEER. You should not be blessed with such a family. The 'Trees' seep like the morning fog. You look up and your dead.

ALISA. That's what you think happened to Janeen.

LAVEER. They contributed their fair share. *(Crosses to the bookcase.)* Life, people and complications.

BABBS. Things would be a lot less complicated for me if I could get the rest of these lyrics ... *(to LAVEER)* Remember that song Janeen used to sing, "Save Me"? *(LAVEER nods.)* Now listen .... *(Singing. Off key.)*
SAVE ME. MISS YOUR LOVIN' ARMS.
YOU CAN SAVE ME. I BEEN CAPTURED BY
 YOUR CHARMS.
COME ON AND SAVE ME. DON'T KNOW WHAT
 TO DO.
'CAUSE I'M... 'CAUSE I'M
Well, help me out.

LAVEER. *(Thinks. Speaking lyrics.)* "Lonely without you. And my world's turned all blue. Tell me, what should I do. 'Cause I'm lonely, lonely, lonely without you. Come on and save me."

BABBS. *(excited)* That's it! *(Singing. Off key.)*
CAUSE I'M LONELY WITHOUT YOU.
AND MY WORLD'S TURNED ALL BLUE.
TELL ME, WHAT SHOULD I DO.

'CAUSE I'M LONELY, LONELY, LONELY WITH-
OUT YOU.
COME ON AND SAVE ME.
I got it!!! Now to make Panzi eat mud. *(She crosses to exit. She quickly turns and retrieves her glass. To ALISA.)* What can I say? I've grown attached to its touch. *(She exits. Silence. LAVEER scans the titles of the books. ALISA crosses to the window.)*

(BABBS can be heard offstage singing "Save Me" off key. THELMA joins her, bringing the song on key and into the right melody. Periodic bursts of laughter interrupt the singing.)

LAVEER. *(listening to the singing)* 'Save Me' ... Could stand for someone to do that ... Alisa .... What do you know about power?

ALISA. It's a great asset when the tenants' rents are due.

LAVEER. I mean ultimate power, the kind which .... *(She snatches a tissue from the tissue box.)* Like this, representing lives. *(She indicates the tissue.)*

ALISA. Whose lives?

LAVEER. *(She thinks, and chooses not to be specific.)* Lives. Power gives you the ability to ..... *(She crumbles the tissue.)* I can do this, with lives, the lives of people I love.

ALISA. Ever thought of leaving the lives right there in the tissue box?

LAVEER. That's all I've been doing lately, thinking, but I'm being pushed. Damn it...Pushed, and pushed too hard...

(Voices can be heard singing offstage. The women are singing the spoof on their alma mater. They sing off key, and in many cases they have forgotten some of the lyrics. There are intermittent intervals of laughter. BABBS can be heard singing off key.)

ALISA. *(listening)* Babbs never could hold a tune.
LAVEER. Neither could Janeen.
ALISA. She said they sang in L sharps and M minors. *(Listens to BABBS.)* That is definitely a L sharp. *(Crosses to LAVEER)* Interesting reading?
LAVEER. A long time ago, yes. Janeen and I used to read passages from this book on the back porch. I can't believe she even remembered the title. Funny what you learn about a person after they're gone.
ALISA. Yes, I guess it is.
LAVEER. I'm partially responsible for what happened.
ALISA. How?
LAVEER. Expected too much from her. Demanded too much. I used to say.... "Janeen! Will you just try something for once. Don't be such a spineless twerp! Try something you want to do! Who's it gonna hurt?" *(to ALISA)* It hurts everyone Alisa. Sometimes there are consequences ..... I remember coaxing Janeen into flipping the swings. Barbara Reeks and I ... we'd done it a thousand times. Pumped the swings as high as we could and then flip them over the top bar.
ALISA. That was good and dangerous.
LAVEER. Who thought of danger. Correction, Janeen thought of the danger. Worried she'd fall, get hurt, her mother'd find out. I called her chicken one time too many and .... The one time she tried, she fell. Blood was everywhere. Her mother had a fit and ..... I just wanted her to be strong, her own person but .... Some people should be left alone. They're consequences for messing with lives. *(She replaces the book on the shelf.)*
ALISA. I think you're being a little too hard on

yourself.

LAVEER. Maybe, maybe not.

ALISA. Well, I'm going to take in a little of this suburban porch sitting. Care to join me?

LAVEER. Later.

ALISA. Okay. Lavy .... don't think too hard on things which were never in your hands. *(She pats LAVEER on the shoulder. ALISA exits.)*

(The lights change. Enter JANEEN.)

JANEEN. The roast ought to be done in a few more moments. *(She stares at LAVEER.)* I'm glad you came. *(She stares at LAVEER in her environment.)* I never could figure out what was missing here. I mean, I bought this and that and that and this and still I kept getting the feeling something was missing .... You.

LAVEER. You flatter me.

JANEEN. I don't. But I have something which may be of interest to you.

LAVEER. What?

JANEEN. *(Crosses to the wall unit and retrieves a small antique box. She crosses to LAVEER with the box.)* This.

LAVEER. And what pray tell is this?

JANEEN. Guess. *(handing LAVEER the box)*

LAVEER. I haven't the foggiest. *(She shakes the box.)* Well what is it?

JANEEN. Patience. *(She crosses to the bookshelf. She removes a book and then retrieves a small key which has been hidden under it. She unlocks the box.)* Okay, open it.

LAVEER. *(Opens the box.)* You're kidding?

JANEEN. No.
LAVEER. These are mine?
JANEEN. Every single strand.
LAVEER. You know I didn't believe you still had these.
JANEEN. Why wouldn't I? You're my friend ..... I'm glad you came. I really am. *(Silence. The two women quietly observe one another.)* You don't feel awkward do you?
LAVEER. Why should I feel awkward?
JANEEN. I don't know, it's been a long time .... a lot of years. Tell me about your life. Are you happy?
LAVEER. Yes.
JANEEN. I like that about you.
LAVEER. What?
JANEEN. The way you can say it all in so few words, "Yes."
LAVEER. I'm a painter. It's the writer who's abundant with words. Why'd you ask if I was happy?
JANEEN. Because I want to know. Gee... can't a friend ask a friend if she's happy or not?
LAVEER. Are you?
JANEEN. What?
LAVEER. Happy?
JANEEN. Sure. Why shouldn't I be? I've got Walter, a home, two cars and a partridge in a pear tree.
LAVEER. Do you love him?
JANEEN. Why ask a question like that?
LAVEER. I want to know.
JANEEN. You're mocking me.
LAVEER. Well ....
JANEEN. On the subject of love. He loves me.

LAVEER. Janeen.

JANEEN. He finally got his practice started, a relief to his family and my mother. I mean now we can start a family and that would make our families very happy.

LAVEER. And what would make you happy?

JANEEN. I am happy.

LAVEER. Do you love him?

JANEEN. *(quickly)* Yes. *(pause)* Really .... I do. I really do.

LAVEER. But ...

JANEEN. Lavy! .... Sometimes I think you can read my mind.

LAVEER. Don't change the subject.

JANEEN. Do I love him? .... Sometimes and sometimes ... Things just didn't turn out the way I thought they would. Like in the books. Remember? I keep waiting for the earth to move, explosions .... something.

LAVEER. Still standing out on the peripheral ... Janeen, you make it move, that is with a little help. Walter ... lousy lover?

JANEEN. No! I mean .... Who do I compare him with? Rayford Jones is hardly anyone to compare anyone with. I've only had two men in my life ... no, I lie, three but the third doesn't count. Three men, isn't that a disgrace?

LAVEER. No.

JANEEN. Lavy!

LAVEER. It's not.

JANEEN. How many men have you had?

LAVEER. Too many to count.

JANEEN. You see.

LAVEER. Three men in your life is not a disgrace. I

should be so lucky.

JANEEN. Really?

LAVEER. Does Walter make you feel good? Now don't lie.

JANEEN. Yes.

LAVEER. He's versatile?

JANEEN. *(embarrassed)* Lavy! .... Yes.

LAVEER. You reach orgasms?

JANEEN. *(embarrassed)* Yes.

LAVEER. Why are you so embarrassed? You're married to the man aren't you?

JANEEN. Yes but ...

LAVEER. But what?

JANEEN. This is embarrassing.

LAVEER. Why?

JANEEN. I don't know. I get this way. On our honeymoon I kept getting this vision of everyone in the church and reception standing around the bed watching us. It was embarrassing.

LAVEER. Why?

JANEEN. I told you, I don't know.

LAVEER. You act like you were a virgin before you married Walter.

JANEEN. Half the world didn't know I was going to make love before I got married. You should see how those people look at you. Even now ... Sometimes, when I'm shopping at the supermarket. One of the Trees will come up to me, look down at my stomach and give me that look which says, "When are you going to put that screwing you and Walter are doing to some use? When are you going to make a baby?" I tell you it's embarrassing.

LAVEER. It shouldn't be. Not if you're in love and you're happy. Why should you care what people think about what you do with your personal life?

JANEEN. I don't know .... I do ....

LAVEER. You're not in love with him.

JANEEN. I am.

LAVEER. Okay.

JANEEN. I am. He's a really sweet man.

LAVEER. And your mother approved of him.

JANEEN. Well, it's important for your parents to approve....

LAVEER. You're not in love with him.

JANEEN. I am. I don't know if he knows that I am, but I am. Lavy, sometimes, when he kisses me it's like ... being in an elevator. You ever get that elevator sensation? I like kissing him.

LAVEER. Liking his kisses is not the same as loving him.

JANEEN. I like talking to him .... I'm just afraid I'm going to fuck things up.

LAVEER. 'Fuck'? .... Janeen said the word 'fuck'?

JANEEN. I know how to swear.

LAVEER. I see. Tell me, why do you think you might fuck things up?

JANEEN. I guess I worry too much about too many things. I guess it's getting in the way.

LAVEER. Tell you what. While you're adding four-letter words to your vocabulary, add a little spunk. The next time you and Walter get together in the sack, and the eyes of all the township are standing around your bed, give them a little show. Screw Walter's ears off, their eyes out and give yourself one hell of a good time. Those visions, they're only visions of your mind, like the boogy man. Remember?

JANEEN. You know why I missed you?

LAVEER. I know, my radiant personality.

JANEEN. No.

LAVEER. What?

JANEEN. I don't know. I just missed you. *(She bursts into her laughter.)* Oh! My roast. Walter should be home any minute and .... I forgot to tell you, he's bringing Julian Ray with him. *(She again bursts into her vibrant laughter.)*

LAVEER. Julian Ray?! ...... Janeen! ......

JANEEN. *(laughing)* What?

LAVEER. Janeen!

JANEEN. *(laughing)* What? *(exits laughing)*

(Lights change back to setting of previous scene. LAVEER replaces the antique box on the bookshelf.)

Scene II

Enter BABBS, high spirited. She carries with her a dessert plate. She stops her stride noticing LAVEER handling the antique box. She assesses the moment and then enters.

BABBS. *(in her anchor person voice)* Good evening. This is Babbs Wilkerson with the Eye Witness News. This evening we are in the suburban community of Ewing Township, New Jersey. Before us is the illustrious and attractive visual artist, Laveer Swan. *(She approaches LAVEER.)* Miss Swan, we are told you fly once a year to partake in the 'Trees' annual German Chocolate Cake Eating Spree.

LAVEER. *(laughs)* Once a year for the ....

BABBS. *(coaxing LAVEER)* Trees annual German Chocolate Cake Eating Spree.

LAVEER. Ah .... Yes. Well .... I certainly try.

BABBS. *(in her anchor person voice)* Our Eye Witness cameras visited the kitchen of this lovely abode and found .... Well ...... *(to imaginary audience)* It is almost unbelievable what this cake does to one's behavior. *(She hands the plate to LAVEER.)* There is a Dr. Thelma Carlson in the kitchen hovering over the cake with a very sharp carving knife ... *(She demonstrates.)* And she has threatened to stab and pierce anyone who attempts to take another slice of this most-delicious cake. *(She fingers a piece of LAVEER's cake. To LAVEER.)* Please tell our viewing audience.... *(She looks into area of imaginary audience.)* Has this always been the affect of your mother's baking?

LAVEER. *(laughs)* Thelma's doing what?

BABBS. *(in her normal voice)* I thought I'd bring you a slice before there wasn't a slice left, or before it was sautéed in blood. This cake brought out the worst in Thelma. *(She steals another small portion of LAVEER's cake.)*

LAVEER. I see she's not the only one who's gotten addicted.

BABBS. What can I say? Your mother can bake her ass off. *(pause)* How are you holding up?

LAVEER. You know me. I always hold up.

BABBS. You've been a little too quiet for me, both you and Panzi. *(Examines the antique box.)* Beautiful.

LAVEER. *(eating the cake)* Yes.

BABBS. Lavy ....

LAVEER. Umm.

BABBS. Tell me if I'm getting out of line, but ... This thing between you and Panzi and Panzi and Walter.

LAVEER. What makes you think there's something between Panzi and Walter?

BABBS. I was there when he gave you the keys and I saw his reaction to Panzi a little earlier in the day.

LAVEER. And your reporter antennae are still operative. Yes?

BABBS. You don't lose the knack simply because you move from the college newspaper to the anchor spot on the evening news. Care to talk?

LAVEER. We are talking.

BABBS. I retreat. Okay? *(Moves about the room admiring the furnishings and decorations.)* I'm told Walter's going to get rid of all of this.

LAVEER. So they say.

BABBS. And he hasn't been back since he found her.

LAVEER. No.

BABBS. Must have really loved her, to react like that.

LAVEER. Different people grieve differently.

BABBS. Grieve ...

LAVEER. Still fishing up a story?

BABBS. No. No. So ... What have you decided about Bahia? Still going?

LAVEER. Maybe in the Spring. What I'd like to do is go home, have a couple of Juan's 'Margarita Bombs', pull out my brightest tubes of reds, yellows, oranges, turquoises, paint and think.

BABBS. About Janeen.

LAVEER. About a lot of things. And yes, Janeen. Jesus you're persistent. *(pause)* I guess you know she called me.

BABBS. I was told.

LAVEER. The day before she washed the pills down with champagne. She as much as announced it. But then how many times had Janeen said ....

(Lights rise on JANEEN.)

JANEEN. I fucked up Lavy. This time I really fucked up. You know what I'd like to do? Close my eyes and start it all over again. *(Lights dim on JANEEN.)*

BABBS. Feeling guilty?

LAVEER. Guilty? .... No. Hurt, yes. You know, I heard it in her voice, the seriousness.

(Lights rise on JANEEN)

JANEEN. I'd like to close my eyes and sleep right through all of this. *(Lights dim on JANEEN.)*

LAVEER. It was as though there was more than desire behind her words, there was the sense of decision. I couldn't shake that sound. Caused me to reroute my ticket and book myself on the first flight coming here. Too late...

BABBS. You tried.

LAVEER. I wonder if they give Brownie points in heaven to all the people who 'tried' but didn't succeed. *(BABBS refills her brandy snifter.)* Ahh, enough of that. When did all this heavy drinking start?

BABBS. We TV world people live highly stressed lives. It's par for the course. *(She drinks.)*

LAVEER. You're going to end up with cirrhosis of the liver.

BABBS. So I get cirrhosis of the liver.

LAVEER. *(pause)* What are you doing to yourself?

BABBS. What am I doing to myself? What haven't I done? ..... I'm thirty-seven, single, divorced, lonely and stuck in a rut. Great subject for a Sunday evening special, hosted by.... 'Babbs Wilkerson'. *(in her anchor person voice)* Good evening. Babbs Wilkerson. Our topic for the evening, "Where are the men of the 'Sixties'?" or .... *(in her normal voice)* "God, I'd just love to run up on one of those fine, spirited, driven, dreamin', doin', basketball playin',

DeBois readin', rhythm and blues lovin', nation buildin', woman lovin', 'Brothers' of the 'Sixties'." *(to LAVEER)* Long on the title huh? *(pause)* I'm still in love with Frank. How many years is it now? And I'm still in love with him.

LAVEER. Ever thought of seeing him? It would save your liver.

BABBS. I did. About a year ago. You know what I found out? I'm not really in love with Frank, but I'm in love with Frank. You see the little Medford, Mass. girl fell in love with that New York Harlem Frank he was in the sixties. Remember the sixties? I'm hooked on midnight navy blue black, six four, suave talking, intelligent, pretty teeth, good kissing, fine loving, 'I'm going to be somebody', nation building, brothers of the sixties. I'm hooked Shit! ... Try to find one today.

(Enter THELMA and PANZI.)

THELMA. Try to find one of what today?

LAVEER. The brothers from the sixties.

THELMA. Who's looking for the brothers from the sixties?

BABBS. I am. *(to LAVEER)* I did a special on our penal system about a year ago. My way of finding out just how many of our men are rotting away in there. You wouldn't believe. Fine ones, kind ones, shy ones ....

PANZI. Sounds like a song to me.

BABBS. Okay... Laugh it off but .... they're in there, all kinds of charges; nickle bags, subversion, being a Panther, being a friend of a Panther. All these fine brothers from the sixties behind bars, my heart ...

THELMA. *(Softly, To LAVEER.)* How'd we get on this?

LAVEER. Frank.

BABBS. You know, I felt good about myself in the sixties. The brothers were men. You didn't have to worry about the color of your skin.

PANZI. She's rhyming again.

BABBS. *(She drinks.)* Damn I miss the sixties. *(to THELMA)* How you ever missed the spirit of the sixties is still beyond me. And the men .... the confidence, drive, determination. That stuff moved mountains. Damn the seventies and eighties ..... Everything's changed. Look at Frank. He's complacent. Harlem, revolutionary Frank .... I need me a man with a mixture. You know? A street wise, book wise, cognac and Budweiser mixture. *(pause)* You think I'll find that in Minneapolis? Maybe I ought to buy a home in Dorchester and work in a community center.

THELMA. Now I know she's drunk.

BABBS. I beg your pardon. I am not drunk. *(crossing to THELMA)* Tell me something Thelma... Now stop me if you think I'm getting out of line but .... You know I always thought you were a beautiful woman. I know what you think, and I think you have a piss poor opinion of your God given ...... *(thinks)* Attributes ....

LAVEER. Come on Babbs, let's go out on the porch for a little air.

BABBS. I don't need any air .... *(to THELMA)* I'm really confused about some things .... And I don't mean to offend you .....

LAVEER. Come on Babbs.

BABBS. I told you, I don't need no air! *(to THELMA)* Where was I? .... Oh yeah .... How did you make it through the sixties and not come out with a better way of feeling about yourself? That was the dawn of Essence. How'd you do it? Dark clothes, thick glasses, corner of the room. I mean that was the time to step forward and shine and you stepped backwards and hid. Why? *(silence)* Would it be too much to ask for an answer?

THELMA. *(silence)* You want an answer? I don't have one. What do you expect? Why is the sky blue? Why is one child to healthy parents born brillant while the other retarded? I don't know. You understand? ... You met my sister, Ava, my brothers, James and Dawson ... You get a good look at them? Hum? .... Could have come from your family, right? Now you look at me. Get yourself a good look at me. *(pause)* In my house, my family .... My people ooh and ahh when a baby is born with light eyes, light hair and God bless the lightest skin possible, your skin....

BABBS. That doesn't say your brothers and sister are more beautiful because ...

THELMA. You did not grow up in my house! You understand? You did not live through the subtleties. I did. I had to be better than everyone. Become a doctor. Did they? .... You don't shake that kind of pain over night. Neither you, the sixties, Martin Luther, Stokely, Rap, Malcolm or a new make over..... *(Indicates her face.)* is going to change what I feel. You don't think I've tried? My mirrors don't reflect back the same reflection as yours.

BABBS. It's not suppose to.

THELMA. In my world it is. Now if that sounds sick, it sounds sick and you'll pardon me if it takes me a little longer to work this thing through. Who knows, I might surprise you. Wake up one morning healed, like in a 'Hands On' service. But right now.... I don't want to talk about it, especially to you. *(She crosses to the door.)* Now, if you don't mind, I'll excuse myself for a little of this northern porch sitting. Maybe the east wind will cleanse me, heal me. I might even return glowing with whatever it is you'd like me to have, but right now I need some air. *(She exits.)*

BABBS. *(silence)* Well .... I guess I fucked up that time, didn't I? Guess this is giving me a bit of cirrhosis of the brain. *(She places the brandy snifter on the table.)* Now to eat crow and beg her forgiveness. *(She crosses to the door and exits. Silence. PANZI and LANEER maintain their perimeter positions.)*

LAVEER. Are you going to continue to grit your teeth, and shoot mental daggers or are you going to get what it is off your chest?

PANZI. You are one nervy bitch. How dare you presume yourself on this moment.

LAVEER. I didn't know I was 'resuming' myself on the moment.

PANZI. What are you doing here?

LAVEER. I thought that was obvious.

PANZI. I resent you being here.

LAVEER. Panzi .... It's been a long four days, an especially longer day today, so if you please ...

PANZI. Just what went on between you and Janeen during her last week?

LAVEER. Not that it's any of your business, a few phone calls.

PANZI. I'm suppose to believe that?

LAVEER. Frankly I don't care what you believe. *(She replenishes her glass.)*

PANZI. A few phone calls and she commits suicide.

LAVEER. Are you implying I had something to do with her suicide?

PANZI. What did you two talk about?

LAVEER. Let's get one thing straight, right now. I am a thirty-eight-year-old woman. It has been some thirty odd years since I was a child, so don't you speak to me in that tone.

PANZI. I want to know what was going on between you and Janeen before ...

LAVEER. You want .... You think I give a good shit about what you want? It was your wants that brought all this to a head in the first place. *(sarcastic mimic)* You want ....

PANZI. What are you getting at?

LAVEER. I am getting at nothing. I am stating facts. Given me via the horse's mouth.

(The lights change. The lights rise on JANEEN.)

JANEEN. *(Meekly. On phone.)* Lavy? ...

LAVEER. Umm humm.

JANEEN. It's me .... Janeen. I was hoping I would catch you. Are you still going to Brazil?

LAVEER. First thing tomorrow morning. *(silence)* Janeen .... Is there something wrong?

JANEEN. I'm pregnant.

LAVEER. Congratulations. *(no response)* You are happy aren't you? *(no response)* Didn't you say you had decided to have ...

JANEEN. He raped me.

LAVEER. Who raped you? *(no response)* Janeen? ... Who raped you?

JANEEN. I don't blame him. I mean, if I had been in his shoes I guess I ....

LAVEER. Janeen, what are you talking about? Who raped....

JANEEN. I didn't mean to hurt him.

LAVEER. Damn it Janeen!

JANEEN. I'd like to just close my eyes, go back to June and change it, but it's not that easy is it?

LAVEER. Who raped you?

JANEEN. Walter.

LAVEER. *(astonished)* Our Walter? Why? *(JANEEN paces and cries.)* Janeen .... Are you still there?

JANEEN. *(meekly)* Yes.

LAVEER. Jesus .... What happened?

JANEEN. I want you to promise me something. Promise me you'll never walk away again .... I'm not sure I can handle all this by myself. Promise me Lavy.

LAVEER. I'm not going anywhere.

JANEEN. Promise you'll stay my friend.

LAVEER. Janeen! ...

JANEEN. Promise!

LAVEER. I promise. Whatever you want me to promise I promise. Now, tell ....

JANEEN. I thought everything was going to bounce

back to normal. Nobody's ever died in my family before. Death.... It changes things. Leaves holes. All of a sudden there were so many holes ... I've been going through a crying binge. I can't seem to stop crying. Like a week or so after Daddy's funeral ... I was walking through the park and all of a sudden I started crying, for no reason, crying, right in the middle of the lawn ....

LAVEER. That's normal Janeen.

JANEEN. I couldn't stop ... Tears everywhere, brought on by everything ... Talk about losing control ... and Walter .... God, it seemed his lecture and conference schedule just picked up. For the first time in our marriage I didn't want him to go. I didn't want him to go. I didn't want to sit here in this silence. I needed him to ... Especially that week-end. I needed him to ... but ... he was giving the opening speech or something and how could I ask him to stay? What grounds did I have? The crazies, a spell of the cries? .... I called Panzi. She canceled week-end plans and came down ....

(Lights change. LAVEER freezes. PANZI participates in the JANEEN/ LAVEER flashback. It is a flashback within a flashback.)

PANZI. You should have called me earlier.

JANEEN. Yes, but ....

PANZI. No buts, you should have called. What are friends for?

JANEEN. I seem to have become such a pest these days.

PANZI. You should have ....

JANEEN. 'Called.' I'm sorry.

PANZI. Just make sure you remember what friends are for, the next time. *(She tastes the caviar.)*

JANEEN. You like? *(Refers to the caviar.)*

PANZI. Not bad.

JANEEN. *(astonished)* Not bad?!

PANZI. It's not bad. What amazes me is how you can have an obsession for caviar and on the other hand be so repulsed by sushi.

JANEEN. Sushi! Raw fish?! .... Yelk ... Ooooouuu .... *(She shrugs her shoulders.)*

PANZI. Janeen, I know a few hundred thousand people who would say... "Fish eggs?! .... Yelk.... Oooooouuuu." *(mimicking JANEEN)*

JANEEN. I have you to know those are not just any 'fish eggs' you are eating there. My dear, what your palate is now enjoying is Russian sturgeon.

PANZI. *(playfully)* My, my .... The good stuff. I'm honored. Champagne .... *(Indicates the bottle.)* and Russian sturgeon. And it's not a wedding reception. To what do I owe the honor?

JANEEN. Friendship.

PANZI. I'm truly horored.

JANEEN. And memory.

PANZI. I see. 'And memory...' Does that mean I'm sharing this with someone, or something else?

JANEEN. Daddy gave them, the champagne and caviar, to Walter and me for our anniversary, a whole case of both. He always had great taste and I thought it would be nice to have some today since I woke up with Daddy, caviar and champagne on the brain. So in honor of your coming ...... *(JANEEN raises her glass. She then crosses to the window. Her mood is that of reflection. She fights tears. Turning to PANZI.)* I'm sorry.... Going through another one of my crying spells .....

PANZI. What are friends for? *(She wraps her arm around JANEEN. The two embrace.)*

JANEEN. You are a good friend. Thanks. *(She touches PANZI's face and then moves away.)* This is all so new ... These feelings .... God, does it ever end?

PANZI. Yeah.

JANEEN. When? Death .... God, it's something you can't prepare yourself for, is it? Did you feel this way when your mother died?

PANZI. My mother? .... *(Crosses away.)* I didn't feel much of anything when she died. She wasn't the kind of woman who'd let a daughter child love her. No, we didn't have the relationship you had with your father.

JANEEN. I feel so empty.

PANZI. It'll pass. It takes its own time.

JANEEN. I hope time is on my side. This is making me crazy. Sometimes, when I'm in here alone.... All of a sudden, out of nowhere I hear Stanley Whiterspoon singing 'Precious Lord' and ...

PANZI. You need to get away.

JANEEN. Where? I can't shut off the voices inside my head, the memories, the emptiness ....

PANZI. You need a fun spot, bright sun, fun, leave your worries behind kind of spot.

JANEEN. What kind of a fun spot?

PANZI. An island, Caribbean, Mediterranean ....

JANEEN. *(Crosses to the antique box. She fingers it.)* I've got just the right place. Hawaii.

PANZI. Now that's the kind I mean.

JANEEN. God, I hadn't thought about that in years. Funny how things make you remember. *(She fingers the box.)* When I was a kid, Lavy and I would take Daddy's Trenton Times, cut it up into strips, tie the paper around our waists and do the hula on the front lawn. There was a time, the only place we ever wanted to visit was Hawaii.

PANZI. You and Laveer?

JANEEN. Umm ...

PANZI. Giving this a little thought, you know there are closer paradise islands. Right off the east coast .....

JANEEN. My mind's made up. Hawaii. I don't think I'll have to work too hard to get Walter to come along. He's due for a vacation. Thanks. *(She pats PANZI as she crosses to the champagne.)* That was a great suggestion. More? *(offering PANZI the champagne)*

PANZI. A little.

JANEEN. Hawaii .... Funny how you forget things. Maybe seeing Lavy helped bring it to the surface.

PANZI. Laveer?

JANEEN. Umm humm.

PANZI. She was here?

JANEEN. Yeah. For Daddy's funeral.

PANZI. That was .... *(calculates)* five months ago.

JANEEN. Yeah.

PANZI. Were you going to tell me or was it a slip of the mouth, a thought out of place?

JANEEN. Yes, but ... I forgot.

PANZI. I see.

JANEEN. Besides talking to you about Lavy isn't the easiest of things, you know. And they were close, Lavy and Daddy. So ... out of deference to him I thought she should know, so I called.

PANZI. I see.

JANEEN. God, Panzi... It's been years since that fall out and people change. She's changed.

PANZI. I see. *(Crosses to the window.)*

PANZI. *(assessing PANZI's mood)* What do you see?

PANZI. What do I see? It's still raining.

JANEEN. Please don't do this? Panzi, I need you to not do this.

PANZI. I didn't know I was *doing* anything.

JANEEN. She's different.

PANZI. I see.

JANEEN. Will you stop saying that? 'I see. I see.'

PANZI. What am I suppose to say? This hurts, you know.

JANEEN. Why? Lavy came up for Daddy's funeral. Why should that hurt you?

PANZI. What did I say when you called me in Switzerland about your father?

JANEEN. You offered to come back to the states.

PANZI. And what did you say? Humm? It wasn't necessary. You'd be alright. Right? .... Was that after you'd contacted Laveer? .... I'm suppose to be your friend, your 'closest friend' as you put it, but what did you do? .... What corner of the world did you pull her out of?

JANEEN. Mexico.

PANZI. Mexico. You call her in from Mexico and tell

me to stay in Switzerland. I feel hurt because ... as a friend, your close friend, I should have been here....

JANEEN. Panzi, Lavy and Daddy were close. Besides Lavy's......

PANZI. If you don't mind, I don't want to discuss Laveer.

JANEEN. I need all of us to be friends again. *(no response)* I've given it a lot of thought. Why can't we leave the arguments and the past in the past? Daddy's death.... It's gotten me to thinking, and asking questions .... We're here on this planet for what, a brief moment? ... All the seconds are important. And I've been asking myself 'What have I done?' 'What have I known?' 'What have I seen, felt?' Having friends around you, who share things with you, they make you feel. Living makes you feel and .... I wonder if Daddy ever lived, ever felt, ever really shared with anyone ... He was so safe ..... Everything done just so, arranged just so ... His life monitored by his parents, the Trees, Momma... I ask myself if *I've* lived, if *I* ever felt anything and ... The times I felt, truly enjoyed ... they were the times I shared with you and Lavy ... God, it seems so long ago, those yesterdays .... Those were the good times.

PANZI. That was a long time ago.

JANEEN. It wasn't about being safe. Remember? Everyone was discovering, finding, trying ..... I should have used those years.... I wish I could have used them ... because.... *(She turns to PANZI.)* I've got great big holes in me and I want them filled again. I know it sounds selfish but.... I feel empty and I want to feel something. I want to enjoy something before I die.

PANZI. What are you really trying to say?

JANEEN. I don't know .... *(She inhales and exhales.)* Walter's not filling them. I mean, he's a nice man. God, please don't get me wrong. He's a good man, a good husband. He's a good person ... He's .... safe. He's not .... passionate. Lacks passion. There's no passion in his living, in what he does ... and that's boring. Ewing Township is boring. My life is boring. Teaching is boring .... And there're these giant holes .... Everyplace, giant holes ... *(She tries to pull herself together.)* I feel whole when I'm with you and Lavy. I wish the two of you could just ... make up. Life was so much fuller when we were back at...

PANZI. You can't go back.

JANEEN. Why?

PANZI. Time moves on. Life changes. People change.

JANEEN. I know but ...

PANZI. Do you understand me? *People* change.

JANEEN. Yes! Lavy's ....

PANZI. I don't want to talk about Laveer! I do not want to talk about Laveer. I'm talking about me ..... about you ..... *(pause)* Janeen .... What do you want from me?

JANEEN. I don't know .... I don't want to be safe anymore.

PANZI. *(Silence. She stares at JANEEN. She checks her watch.)* It's almost show time. I'd better make that popcorn before the film festival starts.

JANEEN. You ever think about the old days, the dorm, late night talks? ... The sentences we didn't have to complete, thoughts we didn't have to translate into words. We kind of just knew ... That strange closeness women have with women.... We just knew... like..... fine tuning. I.... I wanted Walter to sense I needed him here this week-end. He didn't. I didn't want to have to come out and ask him. I wanted him to sense it, know it, like I know when he needs me. He doesn't have to ask. And ... he's not a bad person because he didn't know I needed him. I don't love him less because of it. I just needed him to sense.... I'm just realizing there is a difference between men and women.

PANZI. Yes, there is.

JANEEN. It would be so nice if you and Lavy and I could be close again.

PANZI. Janeen, there was never any true closeness between Laveer and I.

JANEEN. But you wanted it. I know, I saw .... I did try.

PANZI. Yes Janeen, I know, but .... some things you can't force. I learned that from a great one, a great teacher....... my momma. *(pulling herself back to the moment)* Look, I'd better get to that popcorn. We don't want to miss the show, do we?

(The lighting shifts back to previous scene. PANZI freezes.)

JANEEN. You know, that Sunday was strange from the start. The sun and the rain kept doing crazy things. You remember when it rained while the sun was out, we used to say the devil was beating his wife. You remember?

LAVEER. Yes.

JANEEN. We talked, Panzi and me, talked about things I hadn't voiced to anyone before, new revelations .... I mentioned you had come up for Daddy's funeral. That went over like a thunder bolt.

LAVEER. I'm sure it did.

JANEEN. She made popcorn, we opened another bottle of champagne and watched a film festival of Bud Abbot and Lou Costello on the set.... I hadn't laughed in what seemed like years. I remember thinking that while watching Lou get himself into one jam after another and then .... I was crying. I don't even know the transition from laughter to tears. Everything was .... garbled, confused .... And I couldn't stop crying ... the images, thoughts racing through my mind .... Daddy, Walter, new needs, thoughts ..... I missed him, Daddy. I needed Walter ..... *(pause)* She took a hanky and wiped my eyes. I could hear her voice saying everything would be alright, but I couldn't stop crying. She kissed my forehead. I remembered the softness of her kiss and my mind ..... I saw Walter.... For a minute I saw.... She kissed me.... *(silence)* I remember going upstairs. Panzi undressing me. Panzi touching me. Her fingers, the softness ..... Her kisses and .... My mind ..... *(silence)* Say something.

LAVEER. What do you want me to say?

JANEEN. Just say something. Please, don't you be silent. Say something.

LAVEER. What can I say? I'm not going to judge.

JANEEN. I do.... Oh God, I do ..... But for a moment.... I wasn't safe. I didn't care what anyone thought. I finally made a move without consultation and approval and I felt something. I felt .... Then my eyes, my mind ... I couldn't get them out of my eyes .... Reverend Johnson,

Sister Miller, Aunt Louise, Momma, Daddy .... All of them standing around the bed, watching Panzi and me .... Their disappointment ....

LAVEER. Their disappointment is not important, what is, is how you felt.

JANEEN. How I felt? .... God forgive me. I felt good. I needed ..... to be held. I needed arms, kisses .... And her words .....

PANZI. *(to JANEEN)* I need you.

JANEEN. So softly, over and over again ....

PANZI. *(to JANEEN)* I love you.

JANEEN. God forgive me, but I wanted her, that moment, that passion. I felt something and it was good ..... But those eyes hovering over us ... They wouldn't go away ... They wouldn't go away .... And I couldn't run. I couldn't. She was giving me something I needed .... I couldn't run .... I couldn't ..... *(She freezes.)*

(Lights rise on the PANZI and LAVEER scene.)

LAVEER. *(to PANZI)* I know what happened.

PANZI. Just what do you know?

LAVEER. Don't play games with me ... God knows, right now ... I'd serve a long term in hell for what I could do to you. But that won't bring her back, will it? *(no response)* Will it?! *(no response)* Ironically, I don't even care about your sexual preferences.

PANZI. My sexual ....

LAVEER. Believe me, you can screw cows, trees and bumble bees for all I care, but Janeen .... She was not ready for you.

PANZI. I see, you're an authority on Janeen.

LAVEER. I knew her, yes.

PANZI. How well? How well did you know her?

LAVEER. Implying?

PANZI. You're jealous aren't you? You're jealous of what Janeen and I had.

LAVEER. Jealous?

PANZI. I always knew you had a thing for her.

LAVEER. A 'thing' .... If that means friendship, yes.

PANZI. Is that what you call it? I'm straight-forward with mine. Care to come out of your closet?

LAVEER. My closet? .... Panzi. I'm going to set one thing straight with you right now. *If* I had loved Janeen, sexually, I would have loved her. You get what I'm saying? I would have loved her. No pretense. No hiding. No lieing. No desertion. I would have loved her.

PANZI. Really.

LAVEER. That check you can cash, deposit and draw interest on. So you count your blessings I was never your competition.

PANZI. I suppose I should be grateful.

LAVEER. Oh yeah.

PANZI. Pretty sure of yourself.

LAVEER. Undoubtedly. *(pause)* You had no right to do that to her.

PANZI. Do what to her? You act as though she was a child.

LAVEER. In many ways she was.

PANZI. She was a woman and she made a woman's choice.

LAVEER. Janeen never made a choice about anything.

You seduced her with the same tasteless scruples as an old man turning out a young girl.

PANZI. Janeen was a woman.

LAVEER. You're a disgrace.

PANZI. Am I?

LAVEER. And you mock every woman-to-woman relationship based on love and respect.

PANZI. I loved Janeen.

LAVEER. You fucked Janeen. She was nothing more to you than another piece of ass.

PANZI. Really? You know what I think's got you all fluffed out, you wanted her all for yourself.

LAVEER. You're disgusting.

PANZI. Like I said before, jealous. That is the key to all this, isn't it?

LAVEER. The key, the key .... Yes let us deal with the key. These keys .... *(She refers to the house keys.)* You know these, the ones which had you bent out of shape. I think you were distressed at Walter's attitude towards you, why he didn't give these to you. His reason... a scene he happened upon, in his home, in his bed, between his wife and you.

PANZI. I'm suppose to believe that.

LAVEER. Try the process of deduction. Who did he give the keys to?

(Lights rise on JANEEN.)

JANEEN. I didn't see him. Neither did Panzi, but he saw and he changed. Everything changed. I should have known ..... It was weeks before we made love. Weeks of silence, a change in his mood, our eyes never meeting. I should have known ... Then one Sunday morning ... Strange, they've taken on a whole new meaning, Sunday mornings ... He made an announcement, said we were going to make love. Imagine? A command about making love .... He rode me. Hard ... Just took me. Didn't even give me time to put my protection in. Told me not to worry while he pounded away. I kept saying to myself, 'He wants to hurt me' .... I didn't know why, but ... There was no tenderness, no love ... When he finished, he got up, showered, gnarled his mouth and spit the kisses into the basin .... *(pause)* This past Friday I told him I was pregnant. His face .... Emotionless. Walter's face, the man who wanted a house full of children. There was only silence, long silence, the kind that gives headaches. Thick silence.... He told me everything, a replay of every detail he had seen ... I wanted to vomit. I couldn't ... The knot lodged itself in my throat and just sat there torturing me .... He was torturing me .... The silence, his eyes, everything torturing.... You know what he said? "See if Panzi can do that. See if your lady lover can make you a baby."

(Lights dim on JANEEN.)

LAVEER. *(Stares at PANZI. Silence.)* You killed her.
PANZI. Oh did I?
LAVEER. Just as if you poured the champagne and fed her each pill one by one.
PANZI. I see. Let me get this straight. Walter is supposed to have 'walked in on' .... *(She places the phrase in quotation marks.)* Janeen and I.

LAVEER. Unfortunately.

PANZI. And Janeen is suppose to have taken the pills because of this?

LAVEER. Undoubtedly.

PANZI. I'm suppose to buy this?

LAVEER. Totally.

PANZI. You know I don't have to accept this. In fact, I don't have to stand here and listen to you try to put me through a guilt trip. *(She crosses to the door. LAVEER blocks her exit.)* Get out of my way.

LAVEER. When I'm through.

PANZI. You're through now. *(She tries to open the door. LAVEER impedes her.)* I'm going to ask you one more time ...

LAVEER. And then what? And *then* what?! What you gonna do? Huh? You don't frighten me Panzi, so just what are you going to do if I don't let you out the door? *(PANZI forcefully pulls the door ajar. LAVEER once again impedes her. LAVEER pushes.)* Just give me a reason Panzi! Pleeeeeease, just you give me a reason to knock you clean clear 'cross hell and back!

(LAVEER's raised voice and the tussle bring ALISA, BABBS and THELMA in. THELMA assists PANZI. PANZI resists.)

ALISA. *(to LAVEER)* What's going on Lavy?

LAVEER. *(laughs)* "What's going on? ...." You ask what's going on? *(to PANZI)* Care to answer? Hum? Fill them in on all the nice sordid details.

PANZI. *(searching)* Where's my purse?

LAVEER. Ahhhhh no. If you think you're going to waltz

out of here, this evening .... before owning up to what you did, you are out of your fucking mind. You got that?

ALISA. *(to LAVEER)* Calm down Lavy.

LAVEER. Calm down? I haven't started yet. Have I Panzi?

PANZI. I don't have anything to discuss with you.

LAVEER. Oh but you do. In fact I think you owe this one to all of us.

PANZI. *(unable to find her purse)* Where's that God damn purse?!!!!!

THELMA. *(handing PANZI the purse)* Here.

PANZI. *(Crosses to the door. LAVEER once again impedes her movement.)* Somebody get this woman out of my path. *(ALISA crosses to LAVEER.)*

LAVEER. *(To ALISA while continuing to look PANZI in the eye, she neither blinks nor flinches.)* Alisa, I have no qualms with you. So please, back off. *(ALISA steps aside. To PANZI.)* Now you tell them. You tell them how you came in here, to this very very house, in this very room and set off an avalanche she couldn't stop. You tell them what sweet, nice Panzi did to Janeen. *(silence)* Don't have the heart do you? Can't live up to your deeds, can you? *(PANZI crosses away.)* I thought not.

THELMA. Will someone please tell me what the hell is going on?

BABBS. I need a drink. *(Crosses to the brandy. She refills her glass and drinks.)*

PANZI. *(Lights a cigarette, crosses to the window and stares out. Silence. Turns to the group of women.)* I want one thing understood. What I do with my life, how I live it needs no sanctioning from any one of you. *(ALISA sits.)* In the name of setting things straight .... Janeen and I were lovers. *(Silence. ALISA exhales slowly. THELMA sits. BABBS stares into her brandy snifter.)* I loved her. I don't expect any of you to understand, but I did love Janeen.

ALISA. We all loved Janeen ...

THELMA. It just didn't manifest itself in the bed.

PANZI. Look, I don't owe you anything. I owe you .... *(She clicks her fingers.)* Nothing!

LAVEER. Right! But what about Janeen? You owed her explanations.... All the 'whys' .... Why that day? Why that moment? After all those *years* of *'platonic friendship'*, why that moment? Why the sudden distance, the immediate silence? And you talk about love? You strung her out, turned her out and dropped her. So much for your love.

PANZI. I did not turn her out.

LAVEER. You left her without the least bit of concern for what you'd done.

PANZI. 'For what I'd done.'

LAVEER. For what you did.

PANZI. Just what did I do? Tell me? Since when is loving someone a crime?

LAVEER. Loving? .... You mock the concept.

PANZI. Why? Because we were both women?

LAVEER. Because she was Janeen.

PANZI. Oh yes, 'sweet, weak, vulnerable, confused Janeen.' Well pardon me if I don't subscribe to that depiction.

ALISA. She was.

PANZI. I would expect you to agree with her. *(Refers to*

LAVEER.) You've got minds like the Bobbsie Twins.

ALISA. If you're working on alienating me, you're off to a good start.

PANZI. The shit I care Alisa. The shit I care what any of you think.

THELMA. What do you care about Panzi?

PANZI. Don't you cross examine me Thelma. None of you in this room have a right to judge me.

ALISA. No one is judging you. Personally, who you screw is of absolutely no concern of mine, truly. What you do is what you do.

PANZI. And ...

ALISA. And? .... Three a.m., when my head is on my pillow, my mind and my soul, they're at peace.

PANZI. *(sarcastically)* So much for not being judgemental. *(She turns to BABBS.)* Babbs?

BABBS. What am I suppose to say? I'm surprised? I'm not.

PANZI. No?

BABBS. I suspected. Not between you and Janeen, but I suspected. I'd even developed a kind of respect for you, liked the way you handled good female platonic relationships. Kind of dispelled my vampire image of lesbians.

PANZI. And now? ....

BABBS. I'm disappointed.

PANZI. Disappointed ..... My how righteous you all are.

ALISA. Don't you try to put us through a guilt trip. In many ways Janeen was a little girl, innocent and naive...

PANZI. Janeen was a woman.

ALISA. And you used her.

PANZI. No, you used her! All of you used her. In your own little blood sucking ways you used her 'innocence', 'naivetee.' Janeen wanted to be a woman. She wasn't weak, vulnerable, innocent or naive. She was a woman finding her own.

THELMA. And you helped her.

PANZI. I gave her what she wanted and needed.

LAVEER. You paint a revealing portrait except you negate the true colors, the blacks and grays ... You asked what we talked about during her last week. You. Sometimes two, three times a day. You. Your distance. Her feeling of being conquered. Where were you? Too busy living?

PANZI. I'm suppose to be the bad guy because I care about my relationship with Arlene?

LAVEER. Janeen had a relationship, a husband, Walter, or have you forgotten?

PANZI. I never asked her to change her life. I never suggested she leave Walter.

LAVEER. What a shame you never sat her down and taught her the rules. Let me fill you in on something. That Sunday, while you were up there rolling around in the sheets ... *(She indicates upstairs.)* After Walter got a bird's eye view of the two of you, he went off. Chose a Sunday and went off, raped her. Later giving her the motive, a vivid account of what he had seen.

ALISA. No.

LAVEER. Then, two weeks ago, after telling him she was pregnant ... *(PANZI is shocked by this news.)* I'm not surprised you didn't know. But she was. And guess how Walter viewed the baby? Guess?!!!! Something you couldn't give her.

ALISA. Oh God ....

LAVEER. Do you know how many lives you've screwed? Do you know what you did to that man? You don't care, do you? I know, I've been watching you. Trying to understand, put the pieces together. It's never been about Janeen, has it? Looking back over the years, you know what I see?

PANZI. I could give a damn about what you see.

LAVEER. Give a damn. You give a damn. Janeen is laying out there in a plot at Ewing Cemetery. You damn well better give a damn.

PANZI. Or what?!

LAVEER. Winning!!! ..... All about winning. Graduation day, Janeen gave me an ultimatum concerning our friendship. You motivated that, orchestrated it. Years of friendship down the drain and why? .... Pawns .... rooks, kings, *queens*.... It was too much Janeen and I had become friends again. You had to top that, had to win. Well you won! You won! How's the victory feel Panzi?!!! Tell me, how's the victory feel?!!!!!

THELMA. STOP IT!!!! JESUS GOD!!! ..... PLEASE!!! ...... Please ..... *(silence)* What's happened to us? Will somebody please tell me what's happened to us? Look at us. Listen to us. All those years of dreaming... The places we thought we'd be, things we thought we'd be doing... And what have we become? Drunks, dykes, nonconformists, crusaders, hiders... *(She crosses to PANZI.)* What you did was wrong. There's no debate on the subject.

What you did with Janeen.... What you do is wrong. It defies what we stood for. It defies the laws of nature, the laws of God and when you defy the laws of God you......

PANZI. Don't you preach to me about God. I know about God and his laws....

THELMA. Do tell ... What God?

PANZI. Your God, a God who abandons.... And one of his laws in particular ..... Exodus twenty, twelve. You know it?

THELMA. I'm not up to game playing with you Panzi.

PANZI. No game playing. Your God set out a law; 'Honor thy father and thy mother: that thy...'

THELMA. Watch it, you're on the verge of being sacrilegious.

PANZI. *(to THELMA)* 'That thy days may be long upon the land which the Lord the God giveth thee.' Some law ... Seems to me your God forgot an important one. 'Parent, honor and love thy children that they may not know pain, may not know hurt, may not be neglected.' *(to ALISA)* You understand the need for that one, don't you Alisa? *(to THELMA)* Did your God simply forget to add this or did it simply not matter? *(to ALISA)* Do you think you were the only child on this green earth to suffer in youth? You don't hold a patent on it! All of us don't grow up to be quite so sanctimonious and perfect!

ALISA. I'm sure ....

PANZI. No! I have the floor! My turn! ... I was born the soul daughter to Adrelline Lucinda McVain. A very beautiful, shapely, silky hair Adrilline Lucinda McVain.

A woman known for her knowledge of beauty secrets .... jewelry. *(She directs 'jewelry' to LA VEER.)* A mother of three; two boys and one girl. A woman who loved men almost as much as her reflection in the mirror. She had to have her ego stroked continually, had to have euphoric adulations gracing her ears never endingly. My mother .... She had four husbands. All legal. Discarded them when they ran out of adjectives to describe her beauty. I used to wonder if she'd divorce me one day, discard me. I had nightmares of my brothers coming down to the breakfast table and finding my chair vacant and momma explaining in her sweet sultry voice ... 'Panzi didn't know how to talk to Momma. Momma don't share her roof with nobody who don't know how to talk to Momma.' We'd heard that many times; after Daddy disappeared, after Daddy Rudolph, Daddy Jimmy, Daddy Mason .... My brothers, they learned early, caught on quickly, how to talk and stroke Momma. They'd hug her, kiss her, stroke her ego .... and she'd repay you well for flattery. Buy you .... presents .... All you had to do was be a man and know how to compliment Momma ..... *(to ALISA)* And you talk of innocence. When my flat chest began to grow, Momma's eyes got colder, her words more bitter. There was no room for a girl child in my momma's house .... When I was nine, I asked Momma for a Susie Walkmate Doll. It was the only thing I wanted for Christmas. I did everything just the way Momma liked them done to get that doll. *(pause)* Christmas Eve morning Momma got a phone call. I knew it was from a man because she took a long lavendar perfume bath after she hung up the phone. She put on her make-up, her satin robe with the fuzzy feathers, her pink high heel slippers ... I knew it was a man by the way her eyes bit into me. I hid when Mr. Jones rang the door bell. I held my head low when he gave my brothers and me presents. I tried to disappear when he told Momma I was growing into a beautiful young lady. I prayed Mr. Jones hadn't messed things up. Christmas morning .... No Susie Walkmate. Her excuse; the store had run out .... Momma never held me. On her dying bed in Mercy hospital, she clutched my brothers' heads to her breasts but never looked at me with those eyes .... *(to LAVEER)* Your eyes. *(to THELMA)* Where was your God and his laws then? Your God did not soothe me. A woman soothed me. She put her arms around me one cool winter evening while I was still young and she loved me, made me feel like I belonged in this world. A woman gave me that. *(to LAVEER)* And Janeen .... That Sunday morning ... She needed these hands ... I understood her. I knew her longing. I'd been there. *(She fights tears.)* I didn't plan for things to .... Why did you have to come back, stir up all the needs, desires, longings for .... replicas? .... At first, it was only friendship I needed, but the more you rejected, the more I wanted and .... You became my sickness. Why couldn't you have just stayed ..... You had to conjure up all that wanting, needing, rejecting ... Cut from the same cloth .... That same beauty, same cutting edge. You and *Momma* ...... Tell me Laveer, what was wrong with me? *What was wrong with me?!!*

LAVEER. Nothing .... I simply don't like you.

PANZI. *(Stares at LAVEER. Silence.)* Just like that. *(LAVEER does not respond. PANZI laughs.)* Just like .... *(to

LAVEER) I got rid of you once, stopped the pain .... Janeen was mine. Things were simple. Why couldn't you have just stayed ....? *(Silence. To ALISA & BABBS.)* I loved Janeen. *(to THELMA)* Don't you think I'd change things if I could? *(THELMA turns away. BABBS places a nearly-full glass of brandy on the table as in affirmation of sobriety.)*

LAVEER. *(Crosses to the wall unit and retrieves the erotica book.)* We used to sit on the back porch, read erotic passages from dirty books ..... She'd sit there all wide eyed, drawn into the rawness .... Yesterday.

(Lights dim. Lights to black.)

CURTAIN

COSTUMES

YOUNG LAVEER, YOUNG JANEEN — 1950's style skirts, blouses, hair ribbons, socks and shoes.

LAVEER SWAN — Artsie, almost sensual, bright mint green and black dress. She is ladden with authentic and interesting jewelry, mostly gold. Black hat, large brim and veil.

ALISA MYERS-REYNOLDS — Suitable attire, dress reflecting one who has attended funeral services. Glasses and stylish, quite feminine, walking cane.

PANZI LEW McVAIN — Tailored suit, appropriate for funeral services.

THELMA CARLSON — Tailored suit, appropriate for funeral services. Thick eye glasses.

BABBS WILKERSON — Tailored suit, appropriate for funeral services. Color scheme is a bit lighter than the other ladies' suits.

JANEEN EARL-TAYLOR — Silk blouse and skirt (1st scene), Silk lounging attire, pants and long jacket (2nd scene), Silk blouse and skirt (3rd scene) *(All three outfits reflect the affluent life of JANEEN EARL-TAYLOR)*

PROPS PRESET

Books on book shelves. They should be: medical, post college and a section on erotica.

Specific book on erotica.

Curtains at window which pull open.

Telephone on bookshelf (upstage).

Small antique box with strands of hair in it.

Key for antique box. (Hidden under a book on the bookshelf)

Mirror on downstage wall, beside bookshelf. (Actors downstage right side)

Box of tissues on end table.

PROPS BROUGHT IN BY ACTRESS'
(in order of entry)

Children's book bags/ attache cases (1950's style, 2 cases)
— YOUNG JANEEN and YOUNG LAVEER

Comb and brush — YOUNG LAVEER

Erotica book, covered with book cover — YOUNG LAVEER

Single stem flowers and programs from the internment — ALL CHARACTERS

Keys — LAVEER

Telephone — JANEEN

Tray of drinks: (2 brandies, 2 white wines, 1 bourbon [all in fine quality glassware]) — PANZI

Tray of munchies: (caviar, crackers, grapes) — ALISA

Crystal decanter of brandy — PANZI

Bottles of: (1 white wine, 1 bourbon) — LAVEER

Chocolate cake on saucer with fork — BABBS

Tray with china coffee pot, cups, saucers, napkins, spoons: (3 cups, 3 saucers, 3 spoons) — THELMA

Tray of caviar, champagne and napkins: (2 champagne glasses, 1 bottle of champagne)

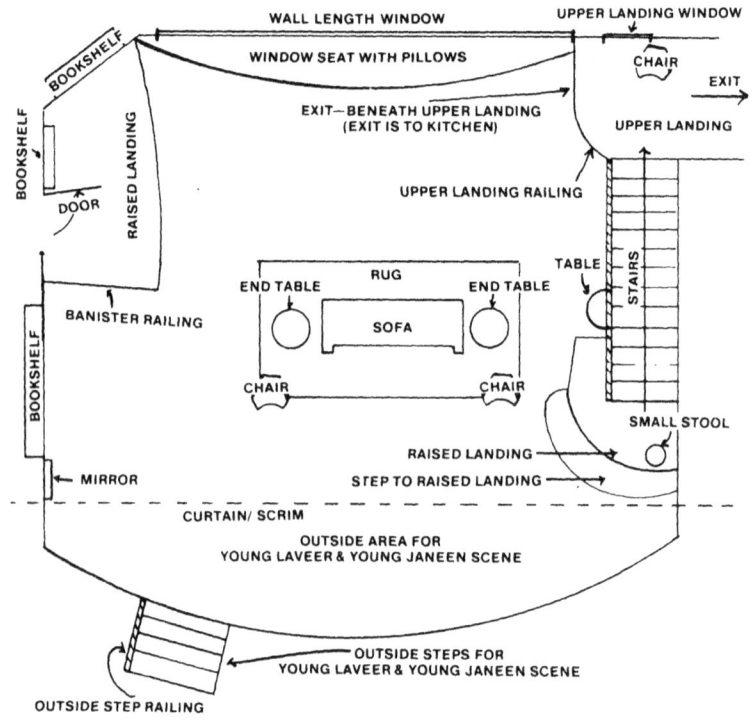

©1986 by Roberta Flack, P.J. Gibson and Paul Griffin.

ANON
Kate Robin

Drama / 2m, 12f / Areaa

Anon. follows two couples as they cope with sexual addiction. Trip and Allison are young and healthy, but he's more interested in his abnormally large porn collection than in her. While they begin to work through both of their own sexual and relationship hang-ups, Trip's parents are stuck in the roles they've been carving out for years in their dysfunctional marriage. In between scenes with these four characters, 10 different women, members of a support group for those involved with individuals with sex addiction issues, tell their stories in monologues that are alternately funny and harrowing..

In addition to Anon., Robin's play What They Have was also commissioned by South Coast Repertory. Her plays have also been developed at Manhattan Theater Club, Playwrights Horizons, New York Theatre Workshop, The Eugene O'Neill Theater Center's National Playwrights Conference, JAW/West at Portland Center Stage and Ensemble Studio Theatre. Television and film credits include "Six Feet Under" (writer/supervising producer) and "Coming Soon." Robin received the 2003 Princess Grace Statuette for playwriting and is an alumna of New Dramatists.

SAMUELFRENCH.COM

WHITE BUFFALO
Don Zolidis

Drama / 3m, 2f (plus chorus)/ Unit Set

Based on actual events, WHITE BUFFALO tells the story of the miracle birth of a white buffalo calf on a small farm in southern Wisconsin. When Carol Gelling discovers that one of the buffalo on her farm is born white in color, she thinks nothing more of it than a curiosity. Soon, however, she learns that this is the fulfillment of an ancient prophecy believed by the Sioux to bring peace on earth and unity to all mankind. Her little farm is quickly overwhelmed with religious pilgrims, bringing her into contact with a culture and faith that is wholly unfamiliar to her. When a mysterious businessman offers to buy the calf for two million dollars, Carol is thrown into doubt about whether to profit from the religious beliefs of others or to keep true to a spirituality she knows nothing about.

www.ingramcontent.com/pod-product-compliance
Lightning Source LLC
Chambersburg PA
CBHW070645300426
44111CB00013B/2266